ALONZO T. J

DUE PROCESS OF LAW

AND THE DIVINE RIGHT OF DISSENT

ADVENTIST PIONEER LIBRARY

Originally published in 1892 by the *The National Religious Liberty Association.*

Published in the USA

May, 2025

ISBN: 978-1-61455-113-3

The original page numbers of the printed edition of this book are found within brackets throughout the text.

ALONZO T. JONES

DUE PROCESS OF LAW

AND THE DIVINE RIGHT OF DISSENT

ADVENTIST PIONEER LIBRARY

"The spirit of the times may alter, will alter. *Our rulers will become corrupt, our people careless. A single zealot may commence persecutor, and better men be his victims. It can never be too often repeated, that the time for fixing every essential right on a legal basis is while our rulers are honest, and ourselves united. From the conclusion of this war we shall be going down hill. It will not then be necessary to resort every moment to the people for support. They will be forgotten, therefore, and* their rights disregarded. *They will forget themselves, but in the sole faculty of making money, and will never think of uniting to effect a due respect for their rights.* The shackles, therefore, which shall not be knocked off at the conclusion of this war, will remain on us long, will be made heavier and heavier, till our rights shall revive or expire in a convulsion."

Thomas Jefferson, *Notes on Virginia*, query XVII.

CONTENTS

INTRODUCTION

❧

Religious legislation is steadily gaining favor in the public mind, and is intrenching itself more and more strongly in the law of the land. In defiance of specific constitutional provisions, in violation of the fundamental principles of American institutions, and contrary to the plain words of Jesus Christ, religious observances are given the sanction of law, and in pursuance thereof are by the power of the State enforced. The chief, the most comprehensive, and the most far-reaching of all these observances is the Sunday, as Blackstone observes, "vulgarly (but improperly) called Sabbath."

From the beginning of our national history, Sunday observance has been enforced by all the original thirteen States. By these it was simply the continuation of the colonial system and legislation, when each of the colonies had an established religion; and from these it has been copied and perpetuated by nearly all the States which in succession have entered the Union. Attempts have also been made to have it copied, established, and enforced by the national Government and authority.

This question has been touched upon several times by both the executive and the legislative branches of the national Government. By the executive branch the action every time has been favorable to the practice; by the legislative branch the action has been decidedly against it. [4] Until 1891, however, the judicial branch of the national Government had never been called upon to take official cognizance of the question. In that year the question of enforced Sunday observance was brought before the Circuit Court of the United States for the Western District of Tennessee, and was acted upon.

This being the first instance of the kind, the action of the court would be worthy of careful consideration, if for no other reason than that it is the first. But in view of the real nature of this action, and the doctrines promulgated by the court in its decision, it is made, for a number of reasons, worthy of the most diligent examination of every American citizen.

CHAPTER 1

THE PROCESS OF LAW

A statement of the case as it came before the court, will be in order. The Constitution of the State of Tennessee, Article I, under the title of "Bill of Rights," declares thus:—

> "Sec. 3. That all men have a natural and indefeasible right to worship Almighty God according to the dictates of their own conscience; that no man can, of right, be compelled to attend, erect, or support any place of worship, or to maintain any ministry against his consent; that no human authority can, in any case whatever, control or interfere with the rights of conscience; and that no preference shall ever be given, by law, to any religious establishment or mode of worship."

Under this strong and specific guaranty, some of the people of that State proposed to exercise their indefeasible right to act in religious things according to the dictates of their own conscience. Among these are some of the sect known denominationally as Seventh-day Adventists. Reading the Bible for themselves, and believing it as they read it, as they [5] have the inalienable and constitutional right to do, they believe, as the fourth of the ten commandments says, that "the seventh day is the Sabbath of the Lord." Holding this as an obligation which they owe to the Lord, they render it to the Lord. Then having rendered to God that which is God's, they exercise their God-given right to work the other six days of the week.

But there are also some people in Tennessee who choose to keep Sunday, as they have the right to do. Yet not content with the exercise of their own right to do this, they desire to compel every one else to do it, whether he believes in it or not. Consequently, several of the Seventh-day Adventists were prosecuted for working on Sunday, after having observed the Sabbath. One of these was Mr. R. M. King, of Obion county. For plowing corn in his own field on Sunday, June 23, 1889, he was prosecuted before the justice of the peace, July 6, and fine and costs were assessed at $12.85, which was collected. This, however, did not satisfy the religious zeal of those who would prohibit the observance of any day but Sunday. But as the only statute on the subject in the State provides only for prosecution "before any justice of the peace of the county;" and provides then only that the person convicted "of doing or exercising any of the common avocations of life" "on Sunday" shall "forfeit and pay *three dollars*," they resorted to extra-statutory measures by which they might execute their arbitrary will. By these measures, if successful, they could have a fine of any amount *above* fifty dollars laid upon any one convicted.

Accordingly, at the July term of the State Circuit Court, Mr. King was indicted by the Grand Jury for Obion county as guilty of the crime of "public nuisance;" "to wit, that he, on the 23rd day of June, 1889, and on divers other Sundays before and after that date, and up to the time of taking this inquisition, in the county of Obion aforesaid, then and there unlawfully and unnecessarily engaged in his secular [6] business, and performed his common avocation of life; to wit, plowing on Sunday, and did various other kinds of work on that day and on Sundays before that day, without regard to said Sabbath days. Said work was not necessary, nor done as a matter of charity, and the doing of said work on said day was and is a disturbance to the community in which done, was offensive to the moral sense of the public, and was and is a common nuisance. So the grand jurors aforesaid present and say that said R. M. King was, in manner and form aforesaid, guilty of a public nuisance by such work on Sunday, etc."

March 6, 1890, the case was brought to trial at Troy, Obion county, before Judge Swiggert. King was convicted, and fined $75 and costs. An appeal was taken to the State Supreme Court. There the judgment was confirmed in a verbal decision, citing a former decision in a like case, in which the judgment was confirmed by declaring Christianity to be part of the common law of Tennessee, and that offenses against it were properly indictable and punishable as common-law offenses.

From this, by writ of habeas corpus, the case was carried before the Circuit Court of the United States for the Western District of Tennessee, upon the plea that the Fourteenth Amendment of the United States Constitution was violated, in that King was deprived of his liberty "without due process of law." The Court was composed of District Judge Hammond and Circuit Judge Jackson. The opinion was written solely by Judge Hammond, and was filed in

Memphis the afternoon of August 1, 1891. It was printed in full in the Memphis Appeal-Avalanche the next day, Sunday, August 2. In the introduction it said: "Judge Hammond says that while he is not authorized to say that Judge Jackson concurs in his opinion, which he has not seen, he does concur in the result and the ground of the decision."

The opinion, as written and printed, is really composed of two parts; namely, the *law* in the case, and the *dictum* of the Judge as to certain questions raised and principles involved in the arguments of counsel for the petitioner.

First, as to the law in the case. The court decided that the proceeding by which King was convicted, was due process of law, because it is exclusively the province of the courts of Tennessee to declare what is the law in that State; and that therefore the only competency possessed by the United States Courts, under such a plea, is to inquire whether the procedure has been regular, and not whether the law itself is lawful.

This deduction is seriously to be questioned in any case; but in *this* case it may not only be seriously questioned but flatly contradicted, because it can be plainly disproved. King's conviction is declared to be in due process of law solely because it is held by the court that it is the prerogative of the Tennessee courts alone to decide what is the law in that State; and when these courts have declared the law, that *is* the law absolutely, and it can neither be reviewed nor questioned in any other court—this, even though the verdict of the jury and the decision of the courts be actually "erroneous." In fact, in this decision the Judge plainly says that if it were within his province to decide the question, he would have "no difficulty in thinking that King was wrongfully convicted," and that there is "not any foundation for the ruling" of the Supreme Court of Tennessee that it is a common-law nuisance to work in one's fields on Sunday." But although he distinctly says that King was wrongfully convicted, and the State Supreme Court "wrongfully decided" when it confirmed his conviction, yet, as it rests exclusively with the State Court to decide what is common law in the State, and as the State Court has decided that such is common law, it does not belong to the United States Court to overrule the State decisions; [8] and therefore he must decide that though the thing was wrongfully done, yet it is "due process of law."

According to this doctrine, it is difficult to see how it would be possible ever to bring a case into any United States Court by virtue of that clause of the Constitution demanding due process of law. For if by any State a person can be "*wrongfully*" deprived of life, liberty, or property, by common-law procedure, and yet it be in "due process of law;" and if the *result* be beyond question or review by any other court, it is hardly to be supposed that the comfort of knowing whether the procedure by which said result was reached was regular or irregular, would be sufficient to induce such unfortunate victim to go to the expense of bringing his case before the United States Court.

CHAPTER 2

CHRISTIANITY AND THE COMMON LAW

B ut whether *this* doctrine of common law be applicable in any other cases or not, it is certain that it is not in any sense applicable in the case here at bar. It is an undeniable principle of the law that the common law is superseded by the written law. A statute repeals the common law on the same subject; and a Constitution supplants the common law on all points upon which the Constitution speaks.

Now 1. As a statute takes the place of the common law on the same subject, and as the State of Tennessee has a statute on the subject of Sunday work, it follows that any indictment or prosecution, at common law, for Sunday work, is therefore precluded, and is void.[1] [9]

2. As a constitution supplants the common law in all points upon which the constitution speaks; as the Constitution of Tennessee expressly declares that "no preference shall ever be given *by law* to any religious establishment or mode of worship;" and as Christianity is in its every intent and purpose a mode of worship; it follows that when the Supreme Court of Tennessee recognized and established Christianity as a part of the common *law* of that State, that Court did thereby positively give preference *by law* to that religion and its modes of worship. But this, being in violation of the express provision of the Constitution, is in itself void.

---

[1] This is not saying nor even admitting that the said statute is either valid or just: it is only saying that where the statute is, procedure by common law or any other means than according to the statute is not due process of law-it is void.

It may be well to give some citations upon this point. The Constitution of California contains substantially the same provisions as does that of Tennessee. And upon this same question the Supreme Court of that State spoke as follows:—

"We often meet with the expression that Christianity is part of the common law. Conceding that this is true, it is not perceived how it can influence the decision of a constitutional question. The Constitution of this State will not tolerate any discrimination or preference in favor of any religion; and *so far as the common law conflicts with this provision, it must yield to the Constitution.* Our constitutional theory regards all religions, as such, equally entitled to protection, and all equally *unentitled to any preference.* Before the Constitution they are all equal. When there is no ground or necessity upon which a principle can rest, but a religious one, then the Constitution steps in and says that you shall not enforce it by authority of law."—*9 Lee 513.*

The Constitution of Ohio has the same provisions, almost word for word, as has the Constitution of Tennessee. And likewise upon this same question the Supreme Court of that State spoke thus:—

"The Constitution of Ohio having declared 'that all men have a natural and indefeasible right to worship Almighty [10] God according to the dictates of conscience; that no human authority can, in any case whatever, control or interfere with the rights of conscience; that no man shall be compelled to attend, erect, or support any place of worship, or to maintain any ministry, against his consent; and that no preference shall ever be given by law to any religious society or mode of worship, and no religious test shall be required as a qualification to any office of trust or profit,' it follows that neither Christianity nor any other system of religion is a part of the law of this State. We sometimes hear it said that all religions are tolerated in Ohio; but the expression is not strictly accurate: much less accurate is it to say that one religion is a part of our law, and all others only tolerated. It is not mere toleration that every individual here is protected in his belief or disbelief. He reposes, not upon the leniency of government, or the liberality of any class or sect of men, but upon his natural, indefeasible rights of conscience, which, in the language of the Constitution, are beyond the control or interference of any human authority."—*2 Ohio Rep., 387.*

The Constitution of New York is substantially the same; and the Supreme Court of that State annihilates the proposition that Christianity is part of the common law, in the following masterly reasoning:—

"The maxim that Christianity is part and parcel of the common law has been frequently repeated by judges and text writers; but few have chosen to examine its truth or attempted to explain its meaning. We have, however, the high authority of Lord Mansfield, and his successor, the present Chief Justice of the Queen's Bench, Lord Campbell, for stating as its true *and only sense*,[2] that the law will not permit the essential truths of revealed religion to be ridiculed and reviled. In other words, that blasphemy is an indictable offense at common law. The truth of the maxim in this very partial and limited sense may be admitted. But if we attempt to extend its application, we shall find ourselves obliged to confess that it is unmeaning or untrue. If Christianity is a municipal law, in the proper sense of the term, *as* [11] *it must be if a part of the common law*, every person is liable to be punished by the civil power, who refuses to embrace its doctrines and follow its precepts. And if it must be conceded that in this sense the maxim is untrue, it ceases to be intelligible, since a law without a sanction is an absurdity in logic and a nullity in fact.

"Let it be admitted, however, that Christianity is a part of the common law, in any sense of the maxim *which those who assert its truth may choose to attribute to it*. The only effect of the admission is to create new difficulties, quite as impossible to overcome as those that have already been stated. How, we would then ask, ... are we to apply the test which Christianity is said to furnish? It will not be pretended that the common law has supplied us with any definition of Christianity. Yet without a judicial knowledge of what Christianity is, how is it possible to determine whether a particular use, alleged to be pious, is or is not consistent with the truths which Christianity reveals?

"No religious use has been or can be created, that does not imply the existence and truth of some particular religious doctrine; and hence, when we affirm the validity of a use as pious, we necessarily affirm the truth of the doctrine upon which it is founded. In a country where a definite form of Christianity is the religion established by law, the difficulty to which we refer is not felt, since the doctrines of the established church then supply the criterion which is sought; *but with us* it can readily be shown that *the difficulty is* not merely real and serious, but *insurmountable*."—*4 Sandford's Superior Court Reports, pp. 181, 182.*

All of this Judge Cooley confirms, in these words:—

"It is frequently said that Christianity is a part of the law of the land.... But the law does not attempt to enforce the precepts of Christianity on the ground of their sacred character or divine origin. Some of these precepts, though we may admit their continual and universal obligation, we must nevertheless recognize as being incapable of enforcement by human laws. That standard of morality which requires one to love his neighbor as himself, we must admit is too elevated to be accepted by human tribunals as the proper test by which to judge the conduct of the citizen; and one could hardly be held responsible to the criminal [12] laws, if in goodness of heart and spontaneous charity he fell something short of the good Samaritan. The precepts of Christianity, moreover, affect the heart and address themselves to the conscience; while the laws of the State can regard the outward conduct only: *and for these several reasons Christianity is not a part of the law of the land in any sense which entitles the courts to take notice of and*

---

[2] We shall see presently, however, that even this sense is not allowable in this country, and that it is not true now, even in England.

base their judgments upon it, except so far as they can find that its precepts and principles have been incorporated in and made *a component part of the positive laws of the State."—Constitutional Limitations, p. 584.*

3. This provision of the Constitution of Tennessee is a part of the title, "Bill of Rights." Now another principle of law and government is that—

"Everything in the declaration of rights contained, is excepted out of the general powers of government, and all laws contrary thereto shall be void."—*Idem., p. 46.*

As therefore the "Declaration of Rights" of the State of Tennessee has provided that "no preference shall ever be given by law to any religious establishment or mode of worship;" as all matters of conscience, religion, and worship are thereby "excepted out of the general powers of government;" and as "all laws contrary thereto shall be void," it is clearly demonstrated that the preference given to Christianity as by common law in the State of Tennessee, is void.

There is yet another defect in this theory that Christianity is part of the common law. The theory is drawn from the English courts. But "even in England, Christianity was never considered as a part of the common law so far as that for a violation of its injunctions, independent of the established laws of man, and without the sanction of any *positive act of Parliament made to enforce these injunctions,* any man could be drawn to answer in a common law court,"[3] as was done in this case by the courts of the State of Tennessee. [13]

But Judge Hammond himself goes even further than this, and in a communication printed in the *Appeal-Avalanche,* Aug. 30, 1891, shows that "in one of the latest cases in England the Lord Chief Justice pronounced former expressions that Christianity is part of the law of the land, as *dicta,* and not true now."

True enough! It is not true now, and it never was true by any principle of justice or right. We have not space here to go into the details of this thing. It must suffice here simply to observe that it was introduced by fraud, it was established by falsehood, and it has been perpetuated by imposture. And query: As it is "not true now" *in England* that Christianity is part of the law of the land, how can it be true that it is true now in *Tennessee,* which professedly derives the doctrine from England? And further and doubly, How can it be true now in Tennessee in face of the

---

[3] Supreme Court of Delaware. 2 Harrington's Rep. 553, quoted by Stanley Matthews in case of "Cincinnati School Board on Bible in the Public Schools," p. 260.

State Constitution, which expressly prohibits it in the declaration that "no human authority can *in any case whatever* control or interfere with the rights of conscience; and no preference shall *ever* be given *by law* to any religious establishment or mode of worship"?

Thus it is demonstrated by the living principles of American law and government, that the procedure of the Tennessee courts in the case of Mr. King, instead of being of absolute authority, as the United States Circuit Court decided, is absolutely void and of no valid authority at all. And the demonstration is complete, the decision of the United States Circuit Court to the contrary notwithstanding, that Mr. King *was deprived of his liberty and property* "WITHOUT DUE PROCESS OF LAW." [14]

CHAPTER 3

THE BELIEF AND AIM OF THE FOUNDERS OF OUR GOVERNMENT

So much for the *law* of the case, and for the point of law in the decision of the United States Circuit Court. We must now turn to the *dictum* of Judge Hammond upon the principles involved in the arguments of counsel for the petitioner. It will be necessary to enter quite largely into the examination of this, because the positions taken and the propositions set forth by the Judge are so sweeping, and so directly opposed to every principle of American law and government, that it becomes of the first importance to every American citizen to know the position occupied by a United States judge upon the religious rights and liberties of the citizen.

The Judge first very properly observes that—

"It was a belief of Mr. Madison and other founders of our Government that they had practically established absolute religious freedom and exemption from persecution for opinion's sake in matters of religion; but while they made immense strides in that direction, and the subsequent progress in freedom of thought has advanced the liberalism of the conception these founders had, as a matter of fact, they left to the States the most absolute power on the subject, and any of them might, if they chose, establish a creed and a church, and maintain it. The most they did, as they confessed, was to set a good example by the Federal Constitution; and happily that example has been substantially followed in this matter, and by no State more thoroughly than Tennessee."

This is all true, and it is well stated. It *was* the aim of the founders of our national Government to establish absolute religious freedom, and exemption from all persecution on account of religion. It was their purpose to make the separation between religion and the Government complete and total, and so to take away from all, the power to persecute under the Government of the United States. This principle, so far [15] as its practical working was concerned, they were obliged to confine to the national Government, because some of the States at that time had established religions, some even had established churches; and to have attempted at that time to embody in the national Constitution a provision prohibiting any State from applying a religious test as a qualification for office, or from making any law respecting an establishment of religion, would have been only to defeat all hope of establishing a national Government at all. There was already such an extreme jealously of a national power, that it was with the greatest difficulty that it was established as it was; and to have attempted, at the first step, to make it extend to the States in the curtailment of their long-established connection with religion, would have raised such a storm as would have engulfed the whole project of the formation of a national Government.

For these reasons they were compelled to confine this principle, in its practical working, to the national power. But in so doing they designed to set an example worthy of being followed, and which they hoped would be followed, by all the States of the Union. Nor has their hope been disappointed. For so faithfully has the example been followed that, as is well remarked by Judge Cooley upon this specific question,—

"A careful examination of the American Constitutions will disclose the fact that nothing is more fully set forth or more plainly expressed than the determination of their authors to preserve and perpetuate religious liberty, and to guard against the slightest approach toward the establishment of an inequality in the civil and political rights of citizens, which shall have for its basis only their differences of religious belief....

"Those things which are not lawful under any of the American Constitutions may be stated thus:—

"1. Any law respecting an establishment of religion. The legislators have not been left at liberty to effect a union of Church and State, or to establish preferences by law in [16] favor of any one religious persuasion or mode of worship. There is not complete religious liberty where any one sect is favored by the State and given an advantage by law over other sects. Whatever establishes a distinction against one class or sect is, to the extent to which the distinction operates unfavorably, a persecution; and if based on religious grounds, a religious persecution. The extent of the discrimination is not material to the principle; it is enough that it creates an inequality of right or privilege.

"2. Compulsory support, by taxation or otherwise, of religious instruction. Not only is no one denomination to be favored at the expense of the rest, but all support of religious instruction must be entirely voluntary. It is not within the sphere of government to coerce it.

"3. Compulsory attendance upon religious worship. Whoever is not led by choice or a sense of duty to attend upon the ordinances of religion, is not to be compelled to do so by the State. It is the province of the State to enforce, so far as it may be found practicable, the obligations and duties which the citizen may be under or may owe to his fellow-citizens or to society; but those which spring from the relations between him and his Maker are to be enforced by the admonitions of the conscience, and not by the penalties of human laws....

"4. Restraints upon the free exercise of religion according to the dictates of conscience. No external authority is to place itself between the finite being and the Infinite, when the former is seeking to render the homage that is due, and in a mode which commends itself to his conscience and judgment as being suitable for him to render, and acceptable to its object.

"5. Restraints upon the expression of religious belief. An earnest believer usually regards it as his duty to propagate his opinions and bring others to his views. To deprive him of this right is to take from him the power to perform what he considers a most sacred obligation.

"These are the prohibitions which in some form of words are to be found in the American Constitutions, and which secure freedom of conscience and religious worship. No man in religious matters is to be subjected to the censorship [17] of the State or of any public authority."—*Constitutional Limitations, Chap. XIII, par. 1-9.* [1]

Thus, although it be true that the founders of the national Government "left to the States the most absolute power on the subject" [2] of religion and religious establishments, all the States have followed the grand example set by our governmental fathers, and, by the clearest constitu-

---

[1] It is too bad that it is so, but it is so, that in his *comments* following this statement of *principles*, he justifies from *precedents* the violation of the *principles*. This, however, does not affect the principles. The principles are sound, and remain so, notwithstanding the unsound comments.

[2] From inattention to the Constitution, this fact is very widely misunderstood. It is generally supposed that the First Amendment to the national Constitution guarantees the free exercise of religion in the States. But this is a mistake. The powers of the national Constitution are delegated. And the powers not delegated are reserved. The Tenth Amendment declares that "the powers not delegated to the United States by this Constitution, *nor prohibited by it to the States*, are reserved to the States respectively or to the people." Now the First Amendment is an inhibition upon *Congress*, but not upon *the States*. It says that "Congress shall make no law respecting an establishment of religion, or prohibiting the free exercise thereof," but it does *not* say that *no State* shall do so. Therefore so far as this Amendment goes, this power was "reserved to the States respectively." As the States have all, by their own Constitutions, repudiated the exercise of any such power, the guaranty has become universal throughout the Union; but it is not made so by any force that is in the First Amendment. The First Amendment to the national Constitution is of no force at all upon any State. Only the last five Amendments are inhibitions upon the States.

tional provisions, have distinctly repudiated all claim of right to use such power in any case whatever.

But while all this is true of the *Constitutions* of the States, it is not true of the governmental *practice*—and especially of the practice of the judicial branch of the State Governments—under those Constitutions. That is to say, the practice of the governmental authorities on this subject has not been according to the principles declared in the Constitutions. [18] In fact, with a few grand exceptions, the practice has been in violation of the Constitutions rather than in conformity therewith. The course of the State of Tennessee in the case now under consideration, and in others, is a fair illustration of the usual procedure in all the States. And in the consideration of the *dictum* of Judge Hammond, it will be seen that this same baleful practice is followed, and is to be followed if this procedure shall secure such recognition as will establish it as a precedent.

CHAPTER 4

PERSECUTION
JUDICIALLY JUSTIFIED

As already quoted, the Judge says that it was a belief of Madison and other founders of the national Government, that "they had practically established absolute religious freedom and exemption from persecution for opinion's sake in matters of religion;" that in this they set a good example, which has been substantially followed by the States; and that the example has been followed "by no State more thoroughly than Tennessee." Yet in the rest of that same sentence, and throughout all the rest of his *dictum*, he renders definitions and lays down propositions that are not only utterly subversive of every principle of religious freedom, but which do in plain words declare and justify the doctrine of persecution for religious dissent.

In stating what, according to his view, is the true measure of the freedom of religious belief which is contemplated and guaranteed by the Constitution of Tennessee, he says:—

> "Sectarian freedom of religious belief is guaranteed by the Constitution; not in the sense argued here, that King as a Seventh-day Adventist, or some other as a Jew, or yet another as a Seventh-day Baptist, might set at defiance the prejudices, if you please, of other sects having control of legislation in the matter of Sunday observance, but only in [19] the sense that he should not himself be disturbed in the practices of his creed; which is quite a different thing from saying that in the course of his daily labor ... he might disregard laws made in aid, if you choose to say so, of the religion of other sects."

That is to say, a man may belong to a sect, that sect may have a creed, they may practice according to that creed, and may not be disturbed in such practice; but at the same time, they must conform to the "laws made in aid of the religion of other sects," who have "control of legislation."

For instance, a man may be a Baptist, and may practice the precepts of the Baptist creed; but if the Methodists should have control of legislation, they could oblige the Baptists by law to conform to the precepts of the Methodist creed. Or one company of people might be Methodists, another Baptists, another Quakers, and so on; but if the Roman Catholics only had control of legislation, and should enact laws enforcing Roman Catholic doctrines and precepts, then the Baptists, Methodists, Quakers, etc., would all be obliged to conform to the Roman Catholic precepts, as by law required. And although protected in the undisturbed practice of *their own* creeds, none of these dissenting sects would be in any wise at liberty to disregard the laws made in aid of the religion of the Roman Catholic sect.

Such, according to Judge Hammond's view, is the freedom of religious belief guaranteed by the Constitution of Tennessee. But it seems to us that this is hardly the idea of "absolute religious freedom" which the founders of our Government believed they had practically established. That we have not misconstrued the Judge's meaning, is made clear by a further extract, as follows:—

> "If a non-conformist of any kind should enter the church of another sect, and those assembled there were required, every one of them, to comply with a certain ceremony, he could not discourteously refuse because his mode was different, or because he did not believe in the divine sanction of [20] that ceremony, and rely upon this constitutional guaranty to protect his refusal."

This is precisely the measure of freedom of religious belief that was "guaranteed" or allowed under the Puritan theocracy of New England. The Congregational Church had control of legislation. It embodied Congregationalist doctrines in the law, and required every one to conform to them. And every one was required to go to church. The Baptists and Quakers did not believe in the divine sanction of those ceremonies. They therefore refused to comply. Their refusal, of course, was counted "discourteous." This discourtesy was made criminal, because it was indeed a violation of the law. They were first fined, but they refused either to pay the fines or to comply with the required ceremonies. They were then whipped; still they refused. They were then banished, and yet they refused, and the Quakers even refused to be banished. Then they were hanged, and yet those who still lived would not comply with the required ceremonies. *And they had no constitutional guaranty to protect them in their refusal.*

And now, says Judge Hammond, in Tennessee, if a nonconformist of any kind refuses to comply with a certain ceremony required of every one by another sect which has control of legislation, *there is no constitutional guaranty to protect his refusal.* That is to say, according to this view, In Tennessee to-day there is no constitutional guaranty of any freedom of religious belief beyond that which was allowed in New England two hundred and fifty years ago.

And thus would a judge of a United States court throw open the field of legislation to whatever religious denomination may secure control of it, and would justify such denomination in the use of the power thus gained to compel every one to conform to the religious ceremonies in which that sect believes, and which it practices. In fact, the very expressions used contemplate an established religion. The Judge [21] uses the phrase, "If a non-conformist of any kind," etc. The term "non-conformist" implies an established religion, which creates *conformists*, and whoever refuses assent, thereby becomes a "non-conformist." And in view of this *dictum*, such non-conformist has no constitutional guaranty of protection.

The logical deduction from the two extracts which we have here presented is that enforced conformity to religious observances is just. These two extracts would logically justify persecution by any sect that can secure control of legislation. Nor are we left to make this logical deduction ourselves. The Judge himself plainly declares it, as follows:—

> "If the human impulse to rest on as many days as one can have for rest from toil, is not adequate, as it usually is, to secure abstention from vocations on Sunday, one may, and many thousands do, work on that day, without complaint from any source; but if one ostentatiously labors for the purpose of emphasizing his distaste for or his disbelief in the custom, *he may be made to suffer for his defiance* BY PERSECUTIONS, if you call them so, *on the part of the great majority*, who will compel him to rest when they rest."

This is about the clearest statement of the doctrine of persecution that we have ever seen. We have read considerable on the subject of religion and the State. We have read the accounts of persecutions through all the ages from the cross of Christ till this day, and we do not remember any instance in which the doctrine of persecution was positively avowed in words. Enforced religious observance and all those things have been advocated, defended, and justified, of course; but those who did it would not allow that it was persecution. In this day of the nineteenth century, however, and in this case, all pretense of denial is thrown aside, and the doctrine of persecution itself, as such, is distinctly avowed and justified, both in arguments and in words.

The doctrine of persecution is bad enough, in all conscience, when it is advocated as something else than what it [22] really is; but when it is distinctly avowed and justified in so many words, intentionally and by authority, then it is far worse. The doctrine of persecution is bad enough when it is preached by religious bigots under cover of something else; but when it is openly set forth in words, and justified from the judicial bench of the Government of the United States, then it is infinitely worse.

From the extracts here given, it is evident that the freedom of religious belief contemplated in the *dictum* of Judge Hammond, is entirely compatible with a religious despotism. And it is equally evident that the position therein taken, justifies all persecution from the crucifixion of Christ to the case at bar.

And these views are set forth as the legitimate expression of public opinion in Tennessee! That is to say, that public opinion in Tennessee upon the question of religious belief stands just where it stood in New England two hundred and fifty years ago. We are free to say, however, that we do not believe that such is public opinion in Tennessee. We are not ready, just yet, to confess that in Tennessee there has been no progress in this respect within the last two hundred and fifty years. That on the part of certain individuals there has been no such progress we freely admit; but that such is the state of public opinion in that State to-day, we do decidedly doubt. It is in order, however, for the press of Tennessee to speak much more plainly than it has yet done, as to whether Judge Hammond has correctly gauged public opinion, or whether he has mistaken his own views for public opinion, in that State, on the question of the constitutional freedom of religious belief.

The reader may for himself form an estimate of the correctness of Judge Hammond's views, so far as the Constitution of Tennessee itself is concerned, by reading again the extract from that document, quoted near the beginning of this review (page 9). [23]

We might here inquire also, whether Judge Hammond, or anybody else, really believes that the doctrine thus set forth by the judge is in accord with the "belief of Mr. Madison and other founders of our Government that they had practically established *absolute religious freedom and exemption from persecution* for opinion's sake in matters of religion"? and whether in this, either he or the State of Tennessee is indeed thoroughly following the example set by those founders of our Government?

CHAPTER 5

THE INDIVIDUAL RIGHT
OF RELIGIOUS BELIEF

From the foregoing extracts, which are a correct outline of the theory of the whole *dictum*, it is seen that there is no recognition of any such thing as the *individual* freedom of religious belief, the *individual* right of conscience, but of "*sectarian* freedom" only. In the whole discussion there is not the slightest appearance of any such thing as the individual right of conscience or of religious belief. Yet the individual right is the American idea, and is the one that is contemplated in the United States Constitution and in the Constitutions of the States, so far as they have followed the example of the national Constitution.

So entirely is the individual right of religious belief excluded from Judge Hammond's view, that he actually refused to entertain, or give any credit to, a certain plea, because he said the petitioner had not proved that the point was "held as a part of the creed of his sect." His words were as follows:—

> "Although he testifies that the fourth commandment is as binding in its direction for labor on six days of the week as for rest on the seventh, he does not prove that that notion is held as a part of the creed of his sect, and religiously observed as such." [24]

By this it is clear that the Judge's idea of sectarian freedom of religious belief led him to ignore, yea, even to deny, the individual right of religious belief. For in demanding that the prisoner should prove that his plea is held by a sect, and religiously observed as such by that sect; and in refusing to entertain the plea, because the accused had not proved that it was a part of some creed, and was so religiously observed, the court did, in fact, deny the right of the individual to believe for himself, and to practice accordingly, without reference to any creed, or the belief of any sect as such. And this is only to deny the right of individual belief, and of the individual conscience. Such, however, is neither the American nor the Christian principle of the rights of religious belief.

The Christian and the American principle is the *individual right of conscience*,—the right of the individual to think for himself religiously, without reference to any sect, and without any interference on the part of anybody, much less on the part of the Government. The idea of the national Constitution on this point is clearly expressed in the following words of Mr. Bancroft, which have often been quoted, but which cannot be quoted too often:—

> "No one thought of vindicating religion for the conscience of *the individual* until a voice in Judea, breaking day for the greatest epoch in the life of humanity by establishing a pure, spiritual, and universal religion for all mankind, enjoined to render to Caesar only that which is Caesar's. The rule was upheld during the infancy of the gospel for all men. No sooner was this religion adopted by the chief of the Roman empire than it was shorn of its character of universality and enthralled by an unholy connection with the unholy State. And so it continued until the new nation, ... when it came to establish a Government for the United States, refused to treat faith as a matter to be regulated by a corporate body, or having a headship in a monarch or a State. Vindicating the *right of individuality* even in religion, and *in religion above all*, the new nation dared to set the example of accepting [25] in its relations to God the principle first divinely ordained of God in Judea."

And then, as though to emphasize the specific statements thus made, the writer declares that thus "*perfect individuality* is secured to conscience" by the United States Constitution. As a matter of fact, in the realm of conscience there is no other right than the right of the individual conscience. There is no such thing as a collective or corporate conscience. There is no such thing as a sectarian conscience. Conscience pertains solely to the individual. It is the individual's own view of his personal relation of faith and obedience to God, and can exist only between the individual and God. Thus the right of religious belief inheres in *the individual*, and is only the exercise of the belief of the individual as his own thought shall lead him with respect to God and his duty toward God, according to the dictates of his own conscience. And as this is the inherent, absolute, and inalienable right of every individual, as many individuals as may choose to do so have the right to associate themselves together for mutual aid and encouragement.

If Mr. Bancroft's views of the national Constitution, as expressed in the above extract, need any confirmation, it can be furnished to any reasonable extent. It may, indeed, be well to give a few facts further in this line, showing that as Mr. Bancroft has expressed the sense of the Constitution in this respect, so upon this question the Constitution expresses the sense of those who formed it.

During the whole time in which the preliminary steps were being taken toward the formation of the national Constitution, the question of the freedom of religious belief was being thoroughly discussed, and especially by the one man who had more to do with the making of the Constitution than any other single individual, except perhaps George Washington. That man was James Madison.

June 12, 1776, the Virginia Assembly adopted a Declaration [26] of Rights, Section 16 of which contained the following words:—

"That religion, or the duty which we owe to our Creator, and the manner of discharging it, can be directed only by reason and conviction, not by force or violence; and therefore all men are equally entitled to the free exercise of religion, according to the dictates of conscience."

July 4, following, the Declaration of Independence of all the Colonies was adopted. Shortly afterward, the Presbytery of Hanover, aided by the Baptists and the Quakers in Virginia, presented a memorial to the Assembly of Virginia, asking that the Episcopalian Church be disestablished in that State, and that the example set by the Declaration of Independence be extended to the practice of religion, according to Section 16 of the Bill of Rights.

The Episcopalian Church was disestablished, but in its place a move was made to establish a system by which a general tax should be levied in support of the *Christian religion*. Again the Presbytery of Hanover, the Baptists, and the Quakers came up with a strong memorial in behalf of the free exercise of religious belief, according to the dictates of conscience. In this memorial they said:—

"The duty that we owe to our Creator, and the manner of discharging it, can only be directed by reason and conviction, and is nowhere cognizable *but at the tribunal of the universal Judge. To judge for ourselves* and to engage in the exercises of religion agreeably to the dictates *of our* own conscience, is *an inalienable right*, which upon the principles on which the gospel was first propagated, and the reformation from popery carried on, *can never be transferred to another.*"—Baird's *"Religion in America," book III, chap. III, par. 22; or "The Two Republics," p. 686.*

Jefferson and Madison gladly and powerfully championed their cause, yet the movement in favor of the general tax was so strong that it was certain to pass if the question came to a vote. Therefore Madison and Jefferson offered a motion [27] that the bill be postponed to the next Assembly, and that meantime it be printed and circulated among the people. The motion was carried. Then Madison drafted a memorial and remonstrance in opposition to the bill, and this memorial was circulated and discussed more largely among the people than was the bill which it opposed. The following passages are pertinent here:—

"We remonstrate against the said bill: 1. Because we hold it for a fundamental and undeniable truth, that religion, or the duty which we owe to our Creator, and the manner of discharging it, can be directed only by reason and conviction, not by force or violence. The religion, then, of *every man* must be left to the conviction and conscience of *every man*; and it is *the right of every man* to exercise it as these may dictate. This right is in its nature *an unalienable right*. It is unalienable because the opinions of men, depending only on the evidence contemplated in their own minds, *cannot follow the dictates of other men*. It is unalienable also, because what is here a right towards men is a duty towards the Creator. It is the duty of every man to render to the Creator such homage, and such only, as he believes to be acceptable to him. This duty is precedent, both in order of time and in degree of obligation, to the claims of civil society. Before any man can be considered as a member of civil society, he must be considered as a subject of the Governor of the universe; and if a member of civil society who enters into any subordinate association must always do it with a reservation of his duty to the general authority, much more must every man who becomes a member of any particular civil society do it with a saving of his allegiance to the universal Sovereign. We maintain, therefore, that in matters of religion no man's right is abridged by the institution of civil society, and that *religion is wholly exempt from its cognizance*."

"Because, finally, the equal right of every citizen to the free exercise of his religion, according to the dictates of conscience, is held by the same tenure with all our other rights. If we recur to its origin, it is equally the gift of nature; if we weigh its importance, it cannot be less dear to us; if we consult the declaration of those rights 'which pertain to the good people of Virginia as the basis and foundation of government,' [28] it is enumerated with equal solemnity, or rather with studied emphasis. Either, then, we must say that the will of the Legislature is the only measure of their authority, and that in the plenitude of that authority they may sweep away all our fundamental rights; or that *they are bound to leave this particular right untouched and sacred*. Either we must say that they may control the freedom of the press, may abolish the trial by jury, may swallow up the executive and judiciary powers of the State, nay, that they may despoil us of our very right of suffrage, and erect themselves into an independent and hereditary Assembly; or we must say that they have no authority to enact into a law the bill under consideration."—*Blakely's "American State Papers," pp. 27, 38; or "The Two Republics," pp. 687, 692.*

This remonstrance created such a tide of opposition to governmental favors to religion that the bill was not only overwhelmingly defeated, but there was adopted in its place, Dec. 26, 1785, "the Act for establishing religious freedom," declaring that as "Almighty God hath created the mind free, ... all Acts to influence it by temporal punishments or burdens, or by civil incapacitations, tend only to beget habits of hypocrisy and meanness, and are a departure from the plan of the holy Author of our religion, who, being Lord both of body and mind, yet chose not to propagate it by coercions on either, as was in his almighty power to do"; and that—

> "The impious presumption of legislators and rulers, civil as well as ecclesiastical, ... have assumed dominion over the faith of others, setting up their own opinions and modes of thinking as the only true and infallible, and as such endeavoring to impose them on others, hath established and maintained false religions over the greatest part of the world, and through all time.... *Be it therefore enacted by the General Assembly,* That no man shall be compelled to frequent or support any religious worship, place, or ministry whatsoever, nor shall be enforced, restrained, molested, or burdened in his body or goods, nor shall otherwise suffer on account of his religious opinions or beliefs; but that all men shall be free to profess, and by argument to maintain, their opinions in matters of religion, and that the same shall in nowise diminish, enlarge, or affect their civil capacities. [29]

> "And though we well know that this Assembly, elected by the people for the ordinary purposes of legislation, have no power to restrain the Acts of succeeding assemblies, constituted with the powers equal to our own, and that therefore to; declare this Act irrevocable, would be of no effect in law, yet we are free to declare, and do declare, that the rights hereby asserted are of *the natural rights of mankind,* and that if any Act shall be hereafter passed to repeal the present or to *narrow its operation,* such Act will be *an infringement of natural right.*"—*Idem., pp. 23, 26, or Idem., pp. 693, 694.*

Immediately following this splendid campaign, direct steps were taken for the formation of a national Constitution, in which movement Madison was one of the leading spirits; and the experience which he had gained in his campaign in Virginia was by him turned to account in the making of the national Constitution, and appeared in that document, in the clause declaring that "no religious test shall ever be required as a qualification to any office or public trust under the United States." But even this was not sufficient to satisfy the great majority of the people, whose views had been broadened, and whose ideas had been sharpened by the memorable contest and victory in Virginia. Therefore an amendment was demanded by many of the States, more fully declaring the right of religious belief, and as a consequence the very first Congress that ever assembled under the Constitution proposed-and it was adopted, upon the approval of the requisite number of States-that which is now the First Amendment to the national Constitution, declaring that "Congress shall make no law respecting an establishment of religion, or prohibiting the free exercise thereof."

Thus it is demonstrated that the words of Bancroft express precisely the ideas of the national Constitution upon this question, and that the freedom of religious belief contemplated and guaranteed by that Constitution is the *individual* freedom of religious belief, and not in any sense such as Judge Hammond contemplates, and calls "*sectarian* freedom of religious belief." [30]

And from this, it further follows that when the Constitution of Tennessee, following, as Judge Hammond himself says, the example of the national Constitution, declares that "no human authority can in any case whatever control or interfere with the rights of conscience," it means the rights of the *individual conscience*, and in no sense refers to or contemplates any such thing as the rights of a "sectarian" conscience; and that when that same Bill of Rights declares that no preference shall ever be given by law to any religious establishment or mode of worship, it means precisely what it says.

Therefore, nothing can be clearer than that when the Supreme Court of Tennessee gives preference by "common law" to the Christian religion, and its modes of worship, it distinctly violates the Constitution of Tennessee, and invades the rights of the people of Tennessee, as by that Constitution declared. Likewise, nothing can be clearer than that Judge Hammond, in setting forth and defining what he calls "sectarian freedom of religious belief" as the meaning of either the United States Constitution or of the Constitution of Tennessee, misses *in toto* the American idea of freedom of religious belief.

According to the proofs here given, it is evident that Mr. King occupied the American and constitutional position, and asserted and claimed only his constitutional right when he presented the plea which Judge Hammond refused to entertain. And it is equally clear that Judge Hammond exceeded the jurisdiction of a court of the United States when he refused to entertain the plea, and demanded that the prisoner should prove that the point pleaded was a part of some creed, and was religiously practiced by some sect.

Further than this, and as a matter of literal fact, it is but proper and just to say that the sect to which Mr. King belongs not only has no creed, but utterly repudiates any claim of any right to have a creed. The sect to which Mr. King belongs [31] longs occupies the Christian and constitutional ground, and holds the Christian and American idea, that it is every man's right to believe for himself alone, in the exercise of his own individual conscience as directed by the word of God, and to worship accordingly.

Therefore, when the court, either State or United States, demanded that Mr. King should prove that his plea was held as a part of the creed of his sect, it not only demanded what it was impossible for him to prove, but it demanded what he has the inalienable and constitutional right to *refuse to prove.*

CHAPTER 6

IS RELIGIOUS FREEDOM A
CIVIL OR CONSTITUTIONAL
RIGHT IN THE
UNITED STATES?

Another extract, full of meaning and of far-reaching consequences, runs as follows:—

"By a sort of factitious advantage, the observers of Sunday have secured the aid of the civil law, and adhere to that advantage with great tenacity, in spite of the clamor for religious freedom, and the progress that has been made in the absolute separation of Church and State.... And the efforts to extirpate the advantage above mentioned by judicial decision in favor of a civil right to disregard the change, seem to me quite useless. The proper appeal is to the Legislature. For the courts cannot change that which has been done, *however done*, by the civil law in favor of the Sunday observers."

This passage is in perfect harmony with the foregoing extracts. It justifies the believers in any religious observance in securing control of legislation, and in compelling all others to conform to such religious observance. And it denies dissenters any appeal, refuge, or resource, other than to do as the oppressors are already doing—that is, by political means to turn the tables, and themselves become the [32] oppressors. It completely ignores, if it does not specifically deny, any such thing as the individual right of religious belief or of conscience.

The Judge states quite plainly a truth upon which we have always insisted, and which we have endeavored to make plain to all; that is, that the Sunday observers have secured the aid of the civil law, and adhere to that advantage in spite of the clamor for religious freedom, and in spite of the progress which has been made in the absolute separation of Church and State. In other writings and for years, as well as in this review, we have shown, over and over again, and have demonstrated by every proof pertinent to the subject, that the American principle of government is the absolute separation of religion and the State, and that therefore Sunday legislation to any extent whatever is directly opposed to American principles, not only in the abstract, but as specifically defined in the Constitution of the United States, and in the Constitutions of the several States following this example.

We have shown, not only according to the fundamental American principle, but according to the principles and express declarations of Christianity, that religious freedom is the inalienable right of every individual, and that therefore Sunday legislation is not only contrary to American principles, but to the principles and precepts of Christianity itself. And we have abundantly shown that although all this be true, yet the Sunday observers—in utter disregard of the lessons of the whole history of the Christian era, in spite of the principles of the Declaration of Independence and the precepts of the United States Constitution, in defiance of the Christianity which they profess, and in face of the direct statements of Jesus Christ—have not only fastened the iniquitous practice upon almost all the States, but are doing their utmost to turn the national Government and laws also into the same evil tide. [33]

To expose this practice, and the essential evil of the practice, has been our work from the first. Our work has been sneered at. Our opposition to the thing has been counted as fighting a man of straw. Our warnings have been counted as but bugaboo cries. And all this because of "the great enlightenment of this progressive age." And now our proofs, our warnings, and our position stand completely confirmed from a judicial bench of the United States, which not only says that the observers of Sunday hold to their advantage in spite of the arguments for religious freedom, and in spite of all the progress that has been made in the absolute separation of Church and State, but justifies the whole proceeding; and in the face of the Constitution of the United States, and of the State of Tennessee, refuses to relieve a citizen of the United States from this spiteful church oppression, and declares that an effort to obtain a judicial decision in favor of a civil right to disregard an enforced religious observance is "quite useless."

It is therefore certain that so far as the jurisdiction of the United States Court, in which Judge Hammond presides, extends, our warnings and our position in regard to the coming denial of the free exercise of religion in the United States are completely confirmed.

We do not present this as proof that our position is correct; for we have known that just as well from the first day that we took this position, as we know it now; but we present it for the purpose of awakening, if possible, those who have counted our efforts as misdirected, to the *fact* that recognition of the civil right of the free exercise of religious belief is almost, if not altogether, a thing of the past *whenever that question is brought to a positive test.*

"The proper appeal is to the Legislature," says the Judge. Well, suppose Mr. King should make his appeal to the Legislature. And suppose the Legislature, in order to take the broadest and strongest ground that it were possible [34] to take, and to settle the question forever, should enact a law declaring in so many words that in the State of Tennessee "no human authority can in any case whatever control or interfere with the rights of conscience, and no preference shall ever be given by law to any religious establishment or mode of worship." Suppose the Legislature should do this, what would it amount to?—Just nothing at all, and for two reasons:—

First, The whole people of Tennessee, in their State Constitution, their supreme law, which is above the Legislature itself, have already made this declaration. And yet "in spite" of it, the Sunday observers have secured control of legislation, and by this have presumed to interfere with and control the rights of conscience, and to give preference by law to their mode of worship. And if the Legislature should enact a similar or any other law on the subject, they would do the same thing in spite of that. Despising the supreme law, they certainly would not hesitate to despise an inferior law.

Secondly, Any such law would amount to nothing, because the Sunday observers would not only despise and override it, but the courts, both State and United States, so far, are partisans of the Sunday observers, and justify their spiteful procedure. Consequently, if the Legislature were to enact such a law, application of the law would certainly be disputed by the Sunday observers. *And no appeal could be made to the courts*; for the Judge has already decided that an appeal to the court is "quite useless." Any wish or attempt to appeal to the court would therefore be met again by the Judge's *dictum*, "The proper appeal is to the Legislature."

In view of this doctrine, therefore, it is proper to inquire What is either court or Constitution for? If the Legislature is supreme, and if the only proper appeal in any question of rights is to the Legislature, then what is the use of either court or Constitution? This point once more sets forth Judge Hammond's *dictum* as utterly contrary to the American [35] principle of government, and as inculcating in its stead the British principle of the omnipotence of the legislative power. But such is not the American principle. The American principle is the supremacy of the people, not the supremacy of the Government; the omnipotence of the people, not of the legislative power.

Rights and liberties belong to the people. In their Constitutions the people have set limits to the legislative power, that the rights of the people may not be invaded. And the State Supreme Courts and the United States Courts are established to stand between the Legislature and the people, and to decide upon the constitutionality of the Acts of the Legislature. In other words, to decide whether the Legislature has kept within the limits which have been set by the people in the provisions of the Constitution; to decide whether the rights of the people have been respected or invaded.

Therefore, as it is the province of the State Supreme Courts, and of the United States Courts, to review the Acts of the Legislature, it follows that these courts are the sources of appeal, and the only sources. The proper appeal, therefore, is not to the Legislature, but to the courts.

The Constitutions of the several States and of the United States declare the rights of the people, as citizens of the United States, and of the several States; and in no case is it proper to appeal to the Legislature in any question as to the rights thus declared. To appeal to the Legislature is in itself to surrender the free exercise of the right; that moment the free exercise of the right is admitted to be a matter to be regulated solely by the majority, and is surrendered entirely to the dictates of the majority.

It is true that this is entirely consistent with the other statements of the Judge's *dictum*, and is in harmony with his view of "sectarian freedom of religious belief;" that is, that the majority may rule in religious things, and that there is no right of dissent from the religious views and opinions [36] enforced by law, in favor of whatever denomination may secure control of legislation. But such is not the American idea of the civil right of dissent.

As we have before proved, the American principle is the principle of the individual right of religious belief; of the individual right of the free exercise of conscience; of the right of the individual to dissent from every religious view of anybody else, and utterly to disregard every religious ceremony, however such ceremony may be regarded by others; the right to refuse to comply with any requirement of any sect, or to conform to any religious ceremony, by whomsoever required. It is the individual right of freedom from any and every provision of law that anybody would invoke for the recognition or enforcement of any religious observance whatever.

This is the right asserted in the Constitution of Tennessee, when it declares that "no human authority can in any case whatever control or interfere with the rights of conscience; and no preference shall ever be given by law to any religious establishment or mode of worship." It is the right asserted in the United States Constitution, where it is declared that "no religious test shall ever be required as a qualification to any office or public trust under the United States," and that "Congress shall make no law respecting an establishment of religion, or prohibiting the free exercise thereof."

Such is the American idea of the individual right to disregard the religious observances of the majority. But when the very courts, both State and United States, which have been established to protect the constitutional rights of the citizen from invasion by an impudent and spiteful majority, abdicate their functions and take the side of the oppressors and justify the oppression, what refuge remains to the citizen? what protection to the minority?—None whatever. Every protective barrier is broken down; every refuge is swept away. [37]

Happily there is yet an appeal to the Supreme Court of the United States. But suppose that court should confirm the doctrine of the Circuit Court, WHAT THEN?[1]

---

[1] An appeal was taken to the Supreme Court; but Mr. King has since died. This ends the present case, but the point in this query is just as important as though Mr. King were yet alive. For other cases will certainly arise, and the question will come before the Supreme Court of the United States at some time.

CHAPTER 7

THE DIVINE RIGHT
OF DISSENT

In the extracts which have so far been given from this *dictum*, there has been no recognition whatever of the right of the individual to differ from the majority in any question of religious belief or observance; no recognition whatever of any right of the individual to think for himself religiously, to believe according to convictions of his own conscience, or to worship according to his belief; *if in such things he disagrees with the religious ideas of the majority, or dissents from the religious observances practiced by the majority.* There is no recognition of any right of dissent.

Nor have the extracts which we have presented, been selected for the purpose of making this feature especially prominent. Indeed, no such thing is necessary, because this is *the* prominent feature of the whole discussion. There is no recognition of any such thing in the whole course of the Judge's opinion. And the source from which this discussion comes, will justify us in presenting further extracts, showing that such is the nature of the discussion throughout.

This characteristic of the discussion is made the more prominent, too, by the fact that the Judge holds constantly that Sunday is *a religious institution,* and its observance is essentially *religious observance.* He gives no countenance [38] whatever to the pretense that has recently been urged by the Sunday-law advocates, that it is "the economical value of the day of rest, and not its religious character, which they would preserve by civil law." His statement as to the nature of Sunday observance is as follows:—

"Sunday observance is so essentially a part of that religion ['the religion of Jesus Christ'] that it is impossible to rid our laws of it."

This again utterly ignores the fact that according to American principles, as declared both in the Constitution of Tennessee and in the United States Constitution, religious observance can never rightly be made a part of the laws, nor any religion recognized by the laws. The supreme law of the United States declares in so many words that "the Government of the United States is not in any sense founded upon the Christian religion." And the Supreme law of Tennessee declares that "no preference shall ever be given by law to *any* religious establishment *or mode of worship*."

Further, this statement, just as far as it is possible for Judge Hammond's authority to go, sanctions that act by which he himself declares that the observers of Sunday have not only secured the aid of the civil law, but continue to hold it, in spite of every demand for religious freedom, and in spite of the progress which has been made in the absolute separation of Church and State. The Judge therefore knows that Sunday legislation is religious legislation, and that the enforcement of Sunday observance is the enforcement of a religious observance. He knows, also, that this is contrary to the individual freedom of religious belief, and that it is contrary to the principle of absolute separation of Church and State; for he plainly says that this "sort of factitious advantage" which the observers of Sunday have secured in the control of the civil law is "in spite of the clamor for religious freedom, and in spite of the progress which has been made in the absolute separation of Church and State," [39]

But as we have seen, he sanctions this pertinacious action of the Sunday observers, and now he justifies the sanction in the following words:—

"Civil or religious freedom may stop short of its logic in this matter of Sunday observance.... Government leaves the warring sects to observe as they will, so they do not disturb each other; *and as to the non-observer, he cannot be allowed* his fullest personal freedom in all respects.... There is scarcely any man who has not had to yield something to this law of the majority, which is itself a universal law *from which we cannot escape in the name of equal rights or civil liberty*."

It may be indeed that men have been, and still are, required to yield something to this law of the majority in matters of religion; yet it is *certainly* true that no such requirement ever has been, or ever can be, just. It is *certainly* true that neither civil nor religious freedom can ever stop short of its logic in any question of religious belief or religious observance.

Religious belief is a matter which rests solely with the individual. Religion pertains to man's relationship to God, and it is the man's personal relationship of faith and obedience, of belief and observance, toward God. Every man has therefore the personal, individual, and inalienable right to believe for himself in religious things. And this carries with it the same personal, individual, and inalienable right *to dissent* from any and every other phase of religious belief that is held by anybody on earth.

This right is recognized and declared by Jesus Christ, not only in the words in which he has commanded every man to render to God that which is God's, while rendering to Caesar that which is Caesar's, but likewise in the following words: "If any man hear my words, and believe not, I judge him not; for I came not to judge the world, but to save the world. He that rejecteth me, and receiveth not my words, [40] hath one that judgeth him: the word that I have spoken, the same shall judge him in the last day." John 12:47, 48.

The word which Christ spoke is the word of God. The one who is to judge, therefore, is God; and in the last day he will judge every man for the way in which he has acted. To this judgment the Lord Jesus refers every man who refuses to believe and rejects his words. If any man hears Christ's words, and believes not, but rejects him and his words, Christ condemns him not, judges him not, but leaves him to the Judge of all, who in the last day will render to every man according to his deeds.

In this, therefore, the Author of Christianity, the Saviour of the world, has clearly recognized and declared the right of every man to dissent from every religion known to mankind, and even from the religion of Christ itself, being responsible only to God for the exercise of that right. He wants every man to believe and be saved, but he will compel none. Christ leaves every man free to receive or reject, to assent or dissent, to believe or disbelieve, just as he chooses: his responsibility is to God alone, and it is the individual who must answer for himself in the last day. "So then every one of us shall give account of *himself* to *God.*" Romans 14:12.

Whoever, therefore, presumes to exercise jurisdiction over the religious belief or observances of any man, or would compel any man to conform to the precepts of any religion, or to comply with the ceremonies of any religious body, or would condemn any man for not believing or complying,—whoever would presume to do any such thing puts himself above Jesus Christ, and usurps the place and the prerogative of God, the Judge of all.

Such is the doctrine of the free exercise of religion, as announced by Jesus Christ himself. And such is the doctrine upon this point that will ever be held by every one who respects that glorious Being. Thus is declared and established [41] by the Author of all true religion, *the inalienable*, the divine, *right of dissent*. And such is the *divine right* of the freedom of religious belief.

Now, as it is the inalienable, the divine, right of every man to dissent from any and every church doctrine, and to disregard every church ordinance, institution, or rite, it follows that whenever the State undertakes to enforce the observance of any church ordinance or institution, it simply makes itself the champion of the church, and undertakes to rob men of their inalienable right to think and choose for themselves in matters of religion. Men are therefore and thereby compelled either to submit to be robbed of their inalienable right of freedom of thought in religious things, or else to disregard the authority of the State. And the man of sound principle and honest conviction will never hesitate as to which of the two things he will do.

When the State undertakes to enforce the observance of any church ordinance or institution, and thus makes itself the champion and partisan of the church, then *the inalienable right* of men *to dissent from* church doctrines and to disregard church ordinances and institutions, *is extended to the authority of the* STATE in so far as it is thus exercised. And that which is true of *church* doctrines, ordinances, and institutions, is equally true of *religious* doctrines and exercises of all kinds.

Nor is this all in this connection. The makers of the Government of the United States recognized this divine right as such, and established the exercise of it as an inalienable *civil* right, "by refusing to treat faith as a matter of government, or as having a headship in a monarch or a State;" by excluding all religious tests; and by forbidding Congress ever to make "any law respecting an establishment of religion, or prohibiting the free exercise thereof." In short, by prohibiting the law-making power from making any law whatever upon the subject of religion. [42]

The people of Tennessee, following this example of the makers of the national Government, established in that State this *divine* right, as also an inalienable *civil* right, by declaring that "no human power can in any case whatever control or interfere with the rights of conscience; and no preference shall ever be given by law to any religious establishment or mode of worship."

And thus "the people of the United States, in harmony with the people of the several States, adopted the principle first divinely ordained by God in Judea."

Therefore, it can never be true in the United States, that either civil or religious freedom may of right stop short of its logic in this matter of Sunday observance, nor in any other matter of religion or religious observance.

Now Sunday as an institution, with its observance, is of the Church only. Its origin and history are religious only. Yet of Sunday observance enforced by law, Judge Hammond speaks thus:—

"The fact that religious belief is one of the foundations of the custom [of Sunday observance] is no objection to it, as long as the individual is not compelled to observe the religious ceremonies others choose to observe in connection with their rest days."

This argument has been made before, by several of the Supreme Courts of the States, but it is as destitute of force as is any other attempt to sustain the Sunday institution. If the argument be legitimate, there is no religious observance known that could not be enforced by law upon all the people, simply by giving the observers of the institution control of legislation. Certain people believe in and practice a certain religious observance, and have sufficient influence to control legislation, enforcing it in their own behalf. Thus the custom is made a part of the law, and as the laws are made presumably for the public good, it is then but a short and easy step to the position that the laws enforcing such observances [43] are for the public good, and not particularly to favor religion; and that *therefore*, though religious belief be the foundation of the custom, and though the observance be in itself religious, this cannot be suffered to be any objection to it, so long as the individual is not compelled to observe other religious ceremonies that have not yet been fixed in the law.

This is all very pretty, and it seems always to have been eminently satisfactory to those who make the argument; for it is not by any means new or peculiar to this day or generation. It is as old as is the contest for the right of the free exercise of religious belief. It was the very position occupied by Rome when the disciples of Christ were sent into the world to preach religious freedom to all mankind. Religious observances were enforced by the law. The Christians asserted and maintained the right to dissent from all such observances; and in fact, from *every one* of the religious observances of Rome, and to believe religiously for themselves, though in so doing they totally disregarded the laws, which, on the part of the Roman State, were held to be beneficial to the population. Then it was held that though religious belief was the foundation of the custom, yet this was no objection to it, because it had become a part of the legal system of the Government, and was enforced by the State for its own good. But Christianity *then* refused to recognize any validity in any such argument.

When paganism was supplanted by the papacy in the Roman empire, the same argument was again brought forth to sustain the papal observances, which were enforced by imperial laws; and through the whole period of papal supremacy, Christianity still refused to recognize any validity whatever in the argument.

Under the Calvinistic theocracy of Geneva, the same argument was again used in behalf of religious oppression. In England the same argument was used against the Puritans and other dissenters, in behalf of religious oppression there. In [44] New England, under the Puritan theocracy, the same argument was used in behalf of religious oppression, and to justify the Congregationalists, who had control of legislation, in compelling the Baptists and the Quakers, under penalty of banishment and even of death, to conform to the religious observances of the Congregationalists. But through it all, Christianity always refused to recognize any validity whatever in the argument, and it always will.

"The rulers of Massachusetts put the Quakers to death and banished the Antinomians and 'Anabaptists,' *not* because of their religious tenets, but because of their *violations of the civil laws.* This is the justification which they pleaded, and it was the best they could make. Miserable excuse! But just so it is: wherever there is such a union of Church and State, heresy and heretical practices are apt to become violations of the civil code, and are punished no longer *as errors in religion, but infractions of the laws of the land.* So the defenders of the Inquisition have always spoken and written in justification of that awful and most iniquitous tribunal."—Baird's "Religion in America," page 94, note.

The truth of the matter is, the fact that religious belief is one of the foundations of the custom is the strongest possible objection that could be made to its being recognized and enforced by the civil power. This is demonstrated by several distinct counts.

1. Jesus Christ has commanded, "Render to Caesar the things that are Caesar's; and to God the things that are God's." In this the Lord has distinctly and positively separated that which pertains to Caesar from that which pertains to God. Things religious are due to God only; things civil are due to Caesar. When the civil power—Caesar—exacts that which is due to God, then it puts itself in the place of God, and so far as this exaction is recognized, God is denied, civil and religious things are confounded, the distinction which Christ has made is practically thrown aside, and the things which he separated are joined together. Upon [45] another subject, he declared, "What God hath joined together, let not man put asunder." And upon this subject it may be declared with equal force, What God hath separated, let not man put together. When the civil power legally adopts a religious custom, and enforces the observance thereof, it does put itself in the place of God. But no power has any right to put itself in the place of

God. Therefore, no civil power can ever of right legally adopt and enforce any religious custom or observance. And wherever such a thing is done, he who regards God the most will respect such action the least.

2. The history of more than eighteen centuries demonstrates that the very worst bane of government is for religionists to have control of the civil power. The legal recognition and enforcement of religious customs, or of customs of which religion is the foundation, is to give religionists control of the civil power just to that extent. And the doing of the thing to *any* extent justifies the doing of it to every conceivable extent. It was this that tortured Christians to death under pagan Rome, and in later centuries under papal Rome. It was this that burnt John Huss at Constance, and Servetus at Geneva; and that whipped and banished the Baptists, and banished and hanged the Quakers, in New England.

The fathers of the American Republic, having before them the whole of this dreadful history, proposed that the people of this nation should be profited by the fearful example, and should be forever free from any such thing. They therefore completely separated the national Government from any connection whatever with religion, either in recognition or in legislation. And in this they set the States the perfect example of human government, which example has been followed in the Constitutions of the States, and by none more thoroughly than by Tennessee.

Yet it has ever been the hardest thing to get the courts of the States to recognize the principle, though distinctly [46] declared in the State Constitutions. And here, in the very first instance in which the United States Court has had opportunity to notice it, instead of the principle's being recognized, it is revolutionized; and instead of the American doctrine of the nineteenth century, the Roman doctrine of the first century is inculcated.

3. We have proved by the express words of Christ, the divine right of dissent in all religious things; that any man has the divine right to dissent from any and every religious doctrine or observance of any body on earth. So long as civil government keeps its place, and requires of men only those things which pertain to Caesar,—things civil,—so long there will be neither dissent nor disagreement, but peace only, between the government and all Christian sects or subjects. But just as soon as civil government makes itself the partisan of a religious party, and sets itself up as the champion of religious observances, just so soon this right of dissent in religious things is extended to the authority of the government, *in so far* as that authority is thus exercised. And so far there will be dissent on the part of every Christian in the government.

Sunday observance is in itself religious, and religious only. The institution is wholly ecclesiastical. The creation of the institution was for religious purposes only. The first law of government enforcing its observance was enacted with religious intent; such has been the character of every Sunday law that ever was made; and such its character is recognized to be in the case at bar in the decision under discussion. The Sunday institution is of ecclesiastical origin only, and its observance is religious only. It is the divine right of every man utterly to ignore the institution, to disregard its observance, and to dissent from the authority which instituted or enjoins it. And when any State or civil government makes itself the partisan of the ecclesiastical body which instituted it, and the champion of the ecclesiastical authority [47] which enjoins it, and enacts laws to compel men to respect it and observe it, this divine right of dissent is then extended to the authority of the government, *so far as it is thus exercised.*

The fact that religious belief is the foundation of the custom, is the one great objection to its observance by any law of any government on earth. And as for the Government of the United States, or of the several States, so entirely is this true, and so certainly and firmly does the principle hold, that even an Act which might otherwise be deemed expedient or valuable as a municipal regulation, would be positively precluded by the Constitution, if it forbade or enjoined any religious observance; that is, if it infringed the free exercise of religion. This point is well stated by the Supreme Court of California in these words:—

"Had the Act been so framed as to show that it was intended by those who voted for it as simply a municipal regulation; yet if, in fact, it contravened the provision of the Constitution securing religious freedom to all, we should have been compelled to declare it unconstitutional for *that* reason."—*9 Lee, 515.*

The *principle* is that it would be impossible for as much damage to accrue to the State or society through the loss of the supposed benefit, however great, as would certainly accrue to both State and society by thus giving to religionists the control of the civil power.

Therefore the simple truth is that that which the Judge pronounces no objection, is in itself the strongest possible objection. "The fact that religious belief is one of the foundations of the custom"—this fact is in itself the one supreme objection which sweeps away every excuse and annihilates every argument that ever can be made in favor of any Sunday law, or in favor of any other law recognizing or enforcing any religious observance, or any custom founded upon any religious observance. [48]

CHAPTER 8

❧ ⬥❧⬥ ❧

IS THIS THE NINETEENTH
CENTURY, OR IS IT
THE FIRST?

Jesus Christ came into the world to set men free, to make known to all mankind the genuine principles of freedom, and of religious freedom above all. The Roman empire then filled the world,—"the sublimest incarnation of power, and a monument the mightiest of greatness built by human hands, which has upon this planet been suffered to appear." That empire, proud of its conquests and exceedingly jealous of its claims, asserted its right to rule in all things, human and divine. As in those times all gods were viewed as national gods, and as Rome had conquered all nations, it was demonstrated by this to the Romans that their gods were superior to all others. And although Rome allowed conquered nations to maintain the worship of their national gods, these, as well as conquered people, were yet considered as only servants of the Roman state. Every religion, therefore, was held subordinate to the religion of Rome, and though "all forms of religion might come to Rome and take their places in their Pantheon, they must come as the servants of the state."

The Roman religion itself was but the servant of the state; and of all the gods of Rome there were none so great as the genius of Rome itself. The chief distinction of the Roman gods was that they belonged to the Roman state. Instead of the state's deriving any honor from the Roman gods, the gods derived their principal dignity from the fact that they were gods of Rome. This being so with Rome's own gods, it was counted at

Rome an act of exceeding condescension to recognize, legally, any foreign god, or the right of any Roman subject to worship any other gods than those of Rome. Neander quotes Cicero as laying down a fundamental maxim of legislation, as follows:— [49]

"No man shall have for himself particular gods of his own; no man shall worship by himself any new or foreign gods, unless they are recognized by the public laws."

Another principle, announced by Maecenas, one of the two chief advisers of Augustus, was this:—

"Worship the gods in all respects according to the laws of your country, and compel all others to do the same, but hate and punish those who would introduce anything whatever alien to our customs in this particular."

Accordingly, the Roman law declared as follows:—

"Whoever introduces new religions, the character and tendency of which are unknown, whereby the minds of men may be disturbed, shall, if belonging to the higher rank, be banished; if to the lower, punished with death."

The Roman empire filled the world. Consequently there was a government ruling over all, in which religion and the state were held to be essentially one and indivisible.

Jesus Christ gathered to himself disciples, instructed them in his heavenly doctrine, bestowed upon them the divine freedom—the soul-freedom—which he alone can give, endued them with power from on high, and sent them forth into the world to preach to every creature this gospel of freedom, and to teach all to observe all things whatsoever he had commanded them.

He had commanded them to render to Caesar only those things that were Caesar's, and to God the things which are God's. This statement was the declaration of the principle of the total separation of religion and the state; and in the mind of every true disciple it was a divine command, inseparable from the divine life, and supported by divine power.

In the exercise of this right the disciples went everywhere, preaching the word, and calling all people to the joy of the salvation of Christ, and to the freedom which that salvation gives. But it was contrary to the principles of Rome. It was actually forbidden by the laws,—laws, too, and principles [50] which were of established usage long before Christ came into the world. The law forbade the introduction of any new religion, but the Christians introduced a new religion. The law especially forbade the introduction of any new religion the tendency of which was to disturb men's minds. Of all religions, the Christian religion appeals most directly and most forcibly to the mind. In the very letter which the apostle Paul wrote to the Christians in Rome, he said to them: "Be not conformed to this world, but be ye transformed *by the renewing of your mind*," and of himself he says, "With *the mind* I myself serve the law of God." The law commanded all to worship the gods according to the law. The Christians refused to worship any of the gods recognized by the law, or any other god but the God revealed in Jesus Christ.

According to Roman principles, the Roman state was divine. Caesar was the embodiment of the Roman state, and was therefore divine. Divine honor was therefore exacted toward the emperor; and, as a matter of fact, the worship of the emperor was the most widespread of any single form of worship known to Rome. He was the chief Roman divinity; accordingly, under the Roman system, that which was due to God was due to Caesar. Consequently, when the Christians refused to render to Caesar the things that were God's, and rendered to him only that which was Caesar's, it was a refusal to recognize in Caesar any attribute of divinity. But as Caesar was the embodiment of the state, to deny to him divinity was to deny likewise divinity to the state.

The preaching of the gospel of Christ, therefore, raised a positive and direct issue between Christianity and the Roman empire. And this was an issue between two principles,—the principle of the freedom of the individual conscience, and therefore the principle of the separation of religion and the state; as against the principle of the union [51] of religion and the state, and therefore the principle of the absolute subjection and enslavement of the individual conscience. Rome refused to recognize the principle of Christianity, and Christianity would not yield the principle. The contest was carried on two hundred and fifty years, through streams of blood and untold suffering of the innocent. Then Rome, by an imperial edict, recognized the justice of the Christian principle, and the right of every man to worship whatever God he pleased, without any interference on the part of the state. The principle of Christianity had triumphed!

Then paganized bishops, ambitious of absolute power, through a dark intrigue with the emperor Constantine, succeeded in establishing a union of the Catholic religion with the Roman state, and thus perverted to the interests of the papacy the victory which had been so nobly won, and again Christianity had to take up the contest in behalf of the rights of conscience, and of the separation of religion and the state. And again through torrents of blood and untold suffering of the guiltless, for more than a thousand years, the papacy made its way to the place of supreme authority in the world.

Then came the Reformation, announcing anew to the world the Christian principle of the absolute separation of religion and the state, and the rights of the individual conscience, and by an unswerving exercise of the divine right of dissent, established Protestantism. But, sad to say, even Protestantism was presently perverted, and the Christian principle was violated which gave it of right a name in the world. Then the contest had still to go on, as ever, through blood and suffering of the innocent, by the Christians' exercise of the divine right of dissent, of the freedom of conscience, and by a protest against a false Protestantism in Geneva, in Scotland, in England, in New England, in Virginia, and all the other American Colonies, except Rhode Island alone. [52]

Then arose the new nation, declaring before all people that "all men are created equal, and are endowed by their Creator with certain unalienable rights, among which are life, liberty, and the pursuit of happiness; that to secure these rights, governments are instituted among men, deriving their just powers from the consent of the governed:" and when the national Government was formed, recognizing and establishing, as an example to all the world, and as a principle of the Government itself, *the Christian principle of the absolute separation of Church and State, and therefore the divine right of the free exercise of the individual conscience;* and requiring of men that they render to Caesar only that which is Caesar's, and leaving them absolutely free to render to God that which is God's, or not to render it at all, even as the individual might choose in the exercise of his own personal individual right of conscience.

Thus, after ages of bloodshed and suffering, through fearful persecution by paganism, Catholicism, and false Protestantism, the Christian principle of freedom of conscience and the separation of religion and the state was made triumphant before all the world.

Much has been said (none too much, however) in praise of the wisdom of the fathers of this Republic in establishing a Government of such magnificent principles; but it would be an impeachment of their common sense to think of them that they could have done any less or any other than that which they did. The history of those ages was before them. They saw the sufferings that had been endured in behalf of the rights of conscience, and which had been inflicted in every instance by religious bigots in control of the civil power. Were they to shut their eyes upon all this, and go blindly blundering on in the same course of suffering and of blood?

Both the history and the philosophy of the whole matter is expressed by Madison in that magnificent memorial and [53] remonstrance which he wrote in behalf of the free exercise of religious belief in Virginia, the principles of which were likewise, by his influence, embodied in the national Constitution. He said:—

"A just government, instituted to secure and perpetuate it [public liberty], ... will be best supported by protecting every citizen in the enjoyment of his religion with the same equality which protects his person and his property; by neither invading the equal rights of any sect, nor suffering any sect to invade those of another.... What a melancholy mark is the bill of sudden degeneracy! Instead of holding forth an asylum to the persecuted, it is itself a signal of persecution. It degrades from the equal rank of citizens all those whose opinions in religion do not bend to those of the legislative authority. Distant as it may be, in its present form, from the Inquisition, it differs from it only in degree. The one is the first step, the other is the last, in the career of intolerance.... Torrents of blood have been spilt in the Old World in consequence of vain hopes of the secular arm to extinguish religious discord by proscribing all differences in religious opinion. Time has at length revealed the true remedy. Every relaxation of narrow and rigorous policy, wherever it has been tried, has been found to assuage the disease. The American theater has exhibited proofs that equal and complete liberty, if it does not wholly eradicate it, sufficiently destroys its malignant influence on the health and prosperity of the State. If, with the salutary effects of this system under our own eyes, *we begin to contract the bounds of religious freedom*, we know no name which will too severely reproach our folly."

The lessons of history were not lost upon the noble minds that formed the Government of the United States. The blood which had been shed, and the sufferings which had been endured, both in the Old World and in the New, bore their fruit in the right of the free exercise of religion, guaranteed by the supreme law of the new nation—the right of every citizen to be protected in the enjoyment of religion with the same just and equal hand that protects his person and his property. This right, in the meaning and intent of [54] those who declared and established it, is the right of "equal and complete liberty," of complete religious freedom, the bounds of which should never be contracted. This is the sense in which the doctrine of the free exercise of religious belief is declared and established by the Constitution of the United States, and by the Constitution of Tennessee and the several States which have followed the example of the national Constitution.

Now, in view of history and these facts, please read the following extract from Judge Hammond's *dictum* on the question of religious freedom:—

"This very principle of religious freedom is the product of our religion, as all of our good customs are; and if it be desirable to extend that principle to the ultimate condition that no man shall be in the least restrained, by law or public opinion, in hostility to religion itself, or in the exhibition of individual eccentricities or practices of sectarian peculiarities of religious observances of any kind, or be fretted with laws colored by any religion that is distasteful to anybody, *those who desire that condition must necessarily await its growth into that enlarged application.* But the courts cannot, in cases like this, ignore the existing customs and laws of the masses, nor their prejudices and passions even, to lift the individual out of the restraints surrounding him, because of those customs and laws, *before the time has come* when public opinion [1] shall free all men in the manner desired. Therefore it is that *the petitioner cannot shelter himself just yet behind the doctrine of religious freedom* in defying the existence of a law and its application to him, which is distasteful to his own religious feeling or fanaticism," etc.

Is it possible that the history of eighteen centuries has taught no lesson that can be learned by a court of the United [55] States? Can it be possible that the streams of blood that have been shed, and the fearful sufferings that have been endured, in behalf of the rights of conscience and the free exercise of religion, have been in vain? Do we indeed stand in the first century instead of the nineteenth? And from there are we to "await the growth" of the principle of religious freedom into such an enlarged application that religion and the State shall be separate? and that every man may enjoy the free exercise of religion, according to the individual conscience? Is it true that the time has not yet come when men can be counted free from religious oppression,—free from religious observances enforced by law—enforced, too, "in spite of religious freedom and in spite of the progress that has been made in the absolute separation of Church and State"? Is it true that from such oppression men cannot shelter themselves yet behind the doctrine of religious freedom?

Again, we can only inquire, and in astonishment, too, Has the history of the past eighteen centuries no lesson upon this subject that can be learned by a court of the United States? Have the sufferings through these centuries for this principle all been endured in vain? Has the work of our governmental fathers been utterly in vain? Do we truly live in the nineteenth century and in the United States? or do we live in the first century and in Rome? [56]

---

[1] It is a rather peculiar doctrine in jurisprudence that a court shall gauge its decisions by public opinion. Courts are supposed to construe the law and declare what the law is, rather than to be feeling about to see what public opinion is. Judges are pledged to declare the law and to administer justice, "without fear of punishment or hope of reward," and not to stand in awe of public opinion, nor to decide what public opinion is.

CHAPTER 9

JUDGE HAMMOND AND THE SEVENTH-DAY ADVENTISTS

Another very important, and what would seem a rather peculiar, passage is the following:—

"The petitioner cannot shelter himself just yet behind the doctrine of religious freedom in defying the existence of a law, and its application to him, which is distasteful to his own religious feeling or fanaticism,—that the seventh day of the week, instead of the first, should be set apart by the public for the day of public rest and religious practices. That is what he really believes and wishes, he and his sect, and not that each individual shall select his own day of public rest, and his own day of labor. His real complaint is, that his adversaries on this point have the advantage of usage and custom, and the laws founded on that usage and custom, not that religious freedom has been denied to him. He does not belong to the class that would abrogate all laws for a day of rest, because the day of rest is useful to religion, and aids in maintaining its churches; for none more than he professes the sanctifying influence of the fourth commandment, the literal observance of which, by himself and all men, is the distinguishing demand of his own peculiar sect."

This is an important statement for more reasons than one. It presumes to define for Mr. King, and the people with whom he is religiously connected, just what they really believe and wish. The thing is done, too, in such a way that it appears that the Judge considers himself capable of defining their beliefs and wishes, *according to his own views*, more plainly and more authoritatively than they themselves are able to do.

We say that his statement is the statement of his own views, and not theirs, because we personally know that as a matter of fact the views attributed to them by Judge Hammond are not in any sense the views held by themselves, as is a matter of public record. In other words, we know and are abundantly [57] able to prove, and shall prove, that the statements made by Judge Hammond, as quoted above, are not true in any sense whatever.

As to the belief and wish of Mr. King as an individual, in this respect, we are able to present it in his own words, over his own signature, as the following plainly shows:—

"43 Bond St., New York City, Oct. 6, 1891.

"*Mr. R. M. King,*

"*Lane, Dyer Co., Tenn.*

"Dear Sir,—His Honor, Judge E. S. Hammond, in his decision in your case, made certain statements in regard to your own personal faith as to laws enforcing the observance of the Sabbath which you observe, which, from what I know of yourself and your people, seem certainly mistaken. I send you herewith these statements, numbered separately, with questions annexed, to which I wish you would write your own answers as to your own personal and individual belief.

"Please answer, and return as soon as possible, and oblige,

Truly yours,

"Alonzo T. Jones,

"*Editor American Sentinel.*"

The statements of Judge Hammond and the questions below, were sent to Mr. King, to which he replied as follows:—

"Lane, Tenn., Oct. 11, 1891.

"*Mr. A. T. Jones,*

"*Bond Street, New York City.*

"Dear Sir,—Your letter of the 6th to hand. I will now proceed to answer the questions in regard to the statements made by His Honor, Judge E. S. Hammond, in his decision on my case.

[The *answers* to questions below, are the words of Mr. King.]

"The Judge's statements are as follows:—

"1. 'His own religious feeling or fanaticism [is] that the seventh day of the week, instead of the first, should be set apart by the public for the day of public rest and religious practices.' [58]

"*Question.*—Is this true, or was it ever true in any sense?

"*Answer.*—'This is not true, and never was true in any sense.'

"2. 'This is what he really believes and wishes, he and his sect, and not that each individual shall select his own day of public rest and his own day of labor.'

"*Question.*—(1.) Is this true in any sense? That is, do you 'really believe and wish' what he says you do?

"*Answer.*—'I never did believe or wish for such a thing.'

"(2.) Do you really believe and wish what he says you do not, that is, that 'each individual shall select his own day of public rest and his own day of labor'?

"*Answer.*—'I believe God has set apart the day; but so far as human government is concerned, each individual should be left free to rest or to work.'

"(3.) To the best of your knowledge and belief, is that which the Judge here says, a true statement of the belief and wishes of your sect upon this point?

"*Answer.*—'I never knew of any of my sect believing or wishing for such a thing.'

"3. 'His real complaint is that his adversaries on this point have the advantage of usage and custom, and the laws formed on that usage and custom, not that religious freedom has been denied to him.'

"*Question.*—(1.) Is it true in any sense that your real complaint is that the Sunday observers have the advantage?

"*Answer.*—'It is not.'

"(2.) Is it your real and unqualified complaint that religious freedom has been denied you?

"*Answer.*—'That is the real complaint.'

"4. 'He does not belong to the class that would abrogate all laws for a day of rest.'

"*Question.*—It is presumed that human laws only are here referred to, therefore do you believe in the rightfulness of human laws enforcing a day of weekly rest? or do you indeed believe that all human laws enforcing a day of rest ought to be abrogated?

"*Answer.*—'I believe all laws enforcing a day of rest ought to be abolished.'

"5. 'He professes the sanctifying influence of the fourth commandment, the literal observance of which by himself [59] and all men is the distinguishing demand of his own peculiar sect.'

"*Question.*—(1.) Is it the distinguishing or any other kind of demand, of yourself, that the literal or any other observance of the fourth commandment shall be enforced upon yourself or anybody else by any form of human law?

"*Answer.*—'No, it is not.'

"(2.) To the best of your knowledge and belief, is any such thing the distinguishing or any other kind of demand of your 'own peculiar sect'?

"*Answer.*—'So far as my knowledge goes, it is not. And I don't believe it ever was in any case.'

"Yours truly,
"(*Signed*) R. M. King." [1]

As for the Seventh-day Adventists, as a denomination, or a "sect," or a "peculiar sect," there is something to be said also.

The Seventh-day Adventists have a record upon this subject, which is plain and unmistakable. Nor is it merely a record in the common acceptation of the term. It is a *public* record—public, too, in the sense that it is a part of the record of the Senate of the United States. December 13, 1888, the United States Senate Committee on Education and Labor gave a hearing upon the bill for a national Sunday law, which had been introduced in the Senate by Senator Blair, Chairman of this Committee. At that hearing the Seventh-day Adventists were officially represented. In the argument that was there made by them in the person of their official representative, this very point was brought out clearly and distinctly more than once, and we here present their position as stated in that argument, and as since published by themselves, and which has thus been made open to all who have a mind to read upon the subject. We quote:— [60]

"*Senator Blair.*—Would it answer your objection in that regard, if, instead of saying 'the Lord's day,' we should say 'Sunday'?

"*Mr. Jones.*—No, sir; because the underlying principle, the sole basis, of Sunday is ecclesiastical, and legislation in regard to it is ecclesiastical legislation. I shall come more fully to the question you ask presently.

"Now, do not misunderstand us on this point. We are Seventh-day Adventists; but if this bill were in favor of enforcing the observance of the seventh day as the Lord's day, we would *oppose it just as much as we oppose it as it is now,* for the reason that civil government has nothing to do with *what* we owe to God, or whether we owe *anything* or not, or whether we *pay* it or not.... Therefore, we say that if this bill were framed in behalf of the real Sabbath of the Lord, the seventh day, the day which we observe,— if this bill proposed to promote its observance, or to compel men to do no work upon that day,—*we would oppose it just as strongly as we oppose it now*; and I would stand here at this table and argue precisely as I am arguing against this, and upon the same principle—the principle established by Jesus Christ, that with that which is God's *the civil government never can of right have anything to do.* That duty rests solely between man and God; and if any man does not render it to God, he is responsible only to God, and

---

[1] By a singular coincidence the same number of the *American Sentinel* in which this matter was first printed-Nov. 19, 1891-also announced the death of Mr. King. He died November 10, 1891.

not to any man, nor to any organization or assembly of men, for his failure or refusal to render it to God. And any power that undertakes to punish any man for his failure or refusal to render to God what is God's, puts itself in the place of God. Any government which attempts it, sets itself against the word of Christ, and is therefore antichristian. This Sunday bill proposes to have this Government do just that thing, and therefore I say, without any reflection upon the author of the bill, this national Sunday bill which is under discussion here to-day is antichristian. But in saying this I am not singling out this contemplated law as worse than all other Sunday laws in the world. There never was a Sunday law that was not antichristian, and there never can be one that will not be antichristian.

"*Senator Blair.*—You oppose all the Sunday laws of the country, then?

"*Mr. Jones.*—Yes, sir.

"*Senator Blair.*—You are against all Sunday laws? [61]

"*Mr. Jones.*—Yes, sir; we are against every Sunday law that was ever made in this world, from the first enacted by Constantine to this one now proposed; *and we would be equally against a Sabbath law if it were proposed*; for that would be antichristian, too.

"*Senator Blair.*—State and national, alike?

"*Mr. Jones.*—State and national, sir."

Again:—

"*Senator Blair.*—In other words, you take the ground that for the good of society, irrespective of the religious aspect of the question, society may not require abstinence from labor on the Sabbath, if it disturbs others?

"*Mr. Jones.*—As to its disturbing others, I have proved that it does not. The body of your question states my position exactly.

"*Senator Blair.*—You are logical all the way through, that there shall be no Sabbath.

Again:—

"*Senator Blair.*—I do not see, from what you are stating, but that Christ recognized an existing law, and that it is continuing at the present time. You say that it is one day, and they say that it is another.

"*Mr. Jones.*—But they are after a law to enforce the observance of the first day of the week as the Lord's day, when they confess that the Lord never gave any command in regard to it. The commandment which God gave says that the 'seventh day is the Sabbath.'

"*Senator Blair.*—Is it still the Sabbath?

"*Mr. Jones.*—Certainly, and we keep it; *but we deny the right of any civil government to compel any man either to keep it or not to keep it.*

"*Senator Blair.*—The civil government of the Jews compelled its observance.

"*Mr. Jones.*—That was a theocracy."

Again:—

"*Senator Blair.*—You are entirely logical, because you say there should be no Sunday legislation by State or nation either. [62]

"*Mr. Jones.*—Of course I am logical, all the way through. I want to show you the wicked principle upon which this whole system is founded, and the reason I do this is because the last step is involved in the first one. If you allow this principle and this movement to take the first step, those who get the power will see in the end that *they* take the last step. That is the danger."

Again:—

"*Senator Blair.*—Your proposition is to strike out the Sabbath from the Constitution and condition of society in these modern times?

"*Mr. Jones.*—No, sir.

"*Senator Blair.*—Certainly, *so far as its existence and enactment and enforcement by law are concerned.*

"*Mr. Jones.*—Yes, sir, by civil law."

Again:—

"*Senator Blair.*—You would abolish the Sabbath anyway?

"*Mr. Jones.*—Yes, *in the civil law.*

"*Senator Blair.*—*You would abolish any Sabbath from human practice which shall be in the form of law*, unless the individual here and there sees fit to observe it?

"*Mr. Jones.*—*Certainly*; that is a matter between man and his God."

There was a proposition made to insert an exemption clause, and upon this point we have the following statements:—

"*Senator Blair.*—You care not whether it is put in or not?

"*Mr. Jones.*—*There is no right whatever in the legislation*; and we will never accept an exemption clause as an equivalent to our opposition to the law. It is *not to obtain relief for ourselves* that we oppose the law. *It is the principle of the whole subject of legislation to which we object*; and an exemption clause would not modify our objection in the least.

"*Senator Blair.*—You differ from Dr. Lewis?

"*Mr. Jones.*—Yes, sir; we will never accept an exemption clause, as tending in the least to modify our opposition [63] to the law. *We as firmly and fully deny the right of the State to legislate upon the subject* with an exemption clause as without it....

"*Senator Blair.*—You object to it?

"*Mr. Jones.*—We object to the whole principle of the proposed legislation. We go to the root of the matter, and deny the right of Congress to enact it.

"*Senator Blair.*—You say that the proposed exemption does not make it any better?

"*Mr. Jones.*—Not a bit."

Nor is this the only record in the case. Feb. 18, 1890, the House Committee on District of Columbia gave a hearing on a Sunday bill introduced by Hon. W. C. P. Breckinridge, for the District of Columbia. The Seventh-day Adventists of the District of Columbia were heard before this Committee. From the verbatim report of the speeches made by them that day, we quote again:—

"*Mr. Corliss.*—Mr. Chairman: I have little time for preliminaries, and none for personalities. I have, however, some arguments to present against the bill under consideration, merely pausing to say that I thank the last speaker [Mr. Crafts] for his confession of lack of argument in support of the bill, which he has shown in the fact of his having indulged in personalities the most of the time allowed to him. I can use my time to better advantage. I will use only a half hour, then yield a half hour to Mr. Jones, of New York. Mr. McKee, also, has a brief, which he will present for consideration.

"*The Chairman.*—We desire to know in whose behalf you appear?

"*Mr. Corliss.*—I reside in this city, sir, with my family. I speak in behalf of the Seventh-day Adventist church in Washington, of which I am, at present, the pastor; as a citizen of the United States; and as a resident of this District. I appear, not as has been affirmed before you, *to speak in behalf of a Saturday Sabbath.* Far from it, Gentlemen of the Committee. *If this bill*, No. 3854, *were to have incorporated into it,* instead of 'Sunday, or the first day of the week,' *the words, 'Saturday, or the seventh day of the week,' there is no one who would oppose it stronger than I.* And I would [64] oppose it just as strongly as I do in its present form, for the reason that it is not sectarianism that calls us here to-day; but we see in this bill a principle of religious legislation that is dangerous, not to our liberties in particular, but to the liberties of the nation. For, as you perceive, this bill has an exemption clause providing that 'this Act shall not be construed to apply to any person or persons who conscientiously believe in and observe another day of the week than Sunday as a day of rest.' *This fact gives us more courage to oppose the measure,* because we know that all fair-minded people will be able to see that *our opposition arises from a broader and higher motive than that of self-interest.*"

Again:—

"*Mr. Corliss.*—Mr. Jones has been called here by myself, as pastor of the Seventh-day Adventist church here in Washington. I have called that church together, and by a rising vote they have requested Mr. Jones to appear here on their behalf. Mr. A. T. Jones, of New York City, Editor of the *American Sentinel.*

"*Mr. Jones.*—Mr. Chairman, and Gentlemen of the Committee: I shall devote most of my remarks to the subject which was made so much of by the gentleman who spoke last on the other side [Mr. Crafts], namely, the Seventh-day Adventists, and their opposition to this legislation...."

"Congress can make no law upon the subject of religion without interfering with the free exercise thereof. *Therefore the Seventh-day Adventists*, while observing Saturday, *would most strenuously oppose any legislation* proposing to enforce the observance of that day. That would be an interference with the free exercise of our right to keep that day as the Sabbath. Therefore we come to you to plead for protection. *We do not ask you to protect us by legislation. We do not ask you to legislate in favor of Saturday, not even to the extent of an exemption clause.* We ask you to protect us by refusing to give to these men their coveted power to invade our rights. We appeal to you for protection in our constitutional rights as well as our rights of conscience....

"Gentlemen, It is time for all the people to declare, as *the Seventh-day Adventists decidedly do*, that this nation is, and of right ought to be, free and independent of all ecclesiastical or religious interference, connection, or control." [65]

If any further evidence be required, here it is:—

"43 Bond Street, New York City, Oct. 6, 1891.

'Eld. O. A. Olsen,

"Pres. Gen'l Conf. S. D. Adventists,

"*Battle Creek, Mich.*

"Dear Sir,—In his decision in the case of R. M. King, or rather in his *dictum* appended to that decision, his Honor, Judge E. S. Hammond, of the United States Circuit Court, makes certain statements in regard to the beliefs and wishes of the 'peculiar sect' with which Mr. King is connected religiously,— the Seventh-day Adventists. From my understanding of the views held by this people on this question, I doubt the correctness of the Judge's statements. Therefore I send herewith a copy of the statements, with questions appended, to which I respectfully request that you will write an answer as fully as you may deem proper. By so doing, you will greatly oblige,

Truly yours,

"Alonzo T. Jones,

"*Editor American Sentinel.*"

The statements of the Court are as follows:—

"(1.) 'His [King's] own religious feeling or fanaticism [is] that the seventh day of the week, instead of the first, should be set apart by the public for the day of public rest and religious practices. *This is what he really believes and wishes, he and his sect*, and *not* that each individual shall select his own day of public rest and his own day of labor.'

"*Question.*—Is this true?

"*Answer.*—I have been personally connected with the Seventh-day Adventist denomination for more than thirty years, and I can freely say that no such belief or wish is entertained by this people. Our belief and wish is directly the opposite of that stated by the Judge.

"(2.) 'He professes the sanctifying influence of the fourth commandment, the literal observance of which by himself and all men *is the distinguishing demand of his own peculiar sect.'*

"*Question.*—Is it the distinguishing or any other kind of demand of the Seventh-day Adventist body, that the literal or any other observance of the fourth commandment shall be enforced upon themselves or anybody else, by any form of human laws? [66]

"*Answer.*—It is not. We do *teach*, not *demand*, that ourselves and all men should observe the fourth commandment literally, as God gave it. But this observance must be the free choice of the individual, according to the dictates of his own conscience. (*Signed*)

O. A. OLSEN,

"*Pres. Gen'l Conf. of the Seventh-day Adventists.*

"*Austell, Ga., Oct. 12, 1891.*"

Thus by evidence which cannot be questioned, it is demonstrated that the statements of Judge Hammond as to the belief and wish of the Seventh-day Adventists, are false in every particular. Indeed, if the points made in the argument before the United States Senate Committee, Dec. 13, 1888, had never been made till this 19th day of November, 1891, and were now publicly made for the first time, in direct and intentional refutation of the statements of the Judge, it would not be possible to make them more flatly contradictory to those statements than they are.

But as these points have been matter of public national record, and matter of knowledge to thousands upon thousands of the people, for nearly three years before Judge Hammond set forth his *dictum*, this *fact* leaves him—a judge of a court of the United States—in the unenviable predicament of having, upon a simple question of fact, officially published to the world a series of statements which are not only untrue in themselves, but which public and official records *show* to be untrue, and which thousands upon thousands of the people *know* to be untrue. [67]

CHAPTER 10

Is This a Prerogative of the United States Courts?

The question, however, as to whether these statements are true or false, is a very small matter compared with the *principle* which is involved, and which underlies this action of the Judge: that is, the assumption of the prerogative of defining and passing judgment upon the beliefs and wishes of citizens of the United States.

For convenience, we insert again the passage referred to, italicizing the words which touch the principles:—

"The petitioner cannot shelter himself just yet behind the doctrine of religious freedom in defying the existence of a law and its application to him, which is distasteful to his own religious feeling or *fanaticism*, that the seventh day of the week, instead of the first, should be set apart by the public for the day of public rest and religious practices. *That is what he really believes and wishes, he and his sect*, and *not* that each individual shall select his own day of public rest, and his own day of labor. His *real* complaint is, that his adversaries on this point have the advantage of usage and custom, and the laws founded on that usage and custom, *not* that religious freedom has been denied to him. *He does not belong* to the class that would abrogate all laws for a day of rest, because the day of rest is useful to religion, and aids in maintaining its churches; for none more than he professes the sanctifying influence of the fourth commandment, the literal observance of which, by himself and all men, is the distinguishing demand of his own peculiar sect."

By this it is evident that the Judge has presumed authoritatively to define for Mr. King and the people with whom he is religiously connected, just what their "religious feeling" is, and what they really believe and wish. And it is evident that the Judge considers himself capable of defining for them what their religious feeling is and what they really believe and wish, better than they can do it for themselves; because that which he declares to be their religious feeling [68] and what they really believe and wish, is directly contrary to what they themselves had formerly and officially declared upon the same points precisely.

Nor does the Judge stop here. Having officially declared for them what their religious feeling is, and what they really believe and wish, and so having this point judicially settled, he proceeds to judge their motives, and to declare them "disingenuous,"—"not noble or high-toned; mean, unworthy ... unworthily or meanly artful," in their "demand for religious freedom." And not content with this, he must needs apply to the religious feeling which he has falsely attributed to them, the opprobrious epithet of "fanaticism."

This is a singular proceeding for a court of the United States. It strongly reminds us of certain court proceedings in times past, which are worth recalling in this connection. There are many of them, but two will suffice for this occasion. Jan. 18, 1573, a certain Mr. White, a Puritan, and "a substantial citizen of London, who had been fined and tossed from one prison to another, contrary to law and justice [yet all in "due process of law."—a. t. j.], only for not frequenting his parish church," and for renouncing the Church of England forms and ceremonies, was prosecuted before an English court, the Lord Chief Justice presiding, who was assisted by the Master of the Rolls, the Master of Requests, a Mr. Gerard, the Dean of Westminster, the Sheriff of London, and the Clerk of the Peace. The record is in part as follows:—

"*Lord Chief Justice.*—Who is this?

"*White.*—White, an't please your honor.

"*L. C. J.*—White! as black as the devil!

"*White.*—Not so, my lord; one of God's children....

"*Master of Requests.*—What scriptures have you to ground your conscience against these garments?

"*White.*—The whole Scriptures are for destroying idolatry, and everything that belongs to it.

"*M. Req.*—These things never served to idolatry. [69]

"*White.*—Shough! they are the same which were heretofore used to that purpose.

"*M. Req.*—Where is the place where these are forbidden?

"*White.*—In Deuteronomy and other places; ... and God by Isaiah commandeth us not to pollute ourselves with the garments of the image....

"*Master of the Rolls.*—These are no part of idolatry, *but are commanded by the prince for civil order*; and if you will not be ordered, you show yourself disobedient to the laws.

"*White.*—I would not willingly disobey any law, only I would avoid those things that are not warranted by the word of God.

"*M. Req.*—These things are by an Act of Parliament, and *in disobeying the laws of your country*, you disobey *God.*

"*White.*—I do it not of contempt, but of conscience; in all other things I am an obedient subject.

"*L. C. J.*—Thou art a contemptuous fellow, and will obey no laws.

"*White.*—Not so, my lord: I do and will obey laws, ... refusing but a ceremony out of conscience; ... and I rest still a true subject.

"*L. C. J.*—The Queen's majesty was overseen not to make you of her council, to make laws and orders for religion.

"*White.*—Not so, my lord; I am to obey laws warranted by God's word.

"*L. C. J.*—Do the Queen's laws command anything against God's word.

"*White.*—I do not so say, my lord.

"*L. C. J.*—Yes, marry, do you, and there I will hold you.

"*White.*—Only God and his laws are absolutely perfect; all men and their laws may err.

"*L. C. J.*—This is one of Shaw's darlings. I tell thee what, I will not say anything of affection, for I know thee not, saving by this occasion; thou art the wickedest and most contemptuous person that has come before me since I sat in this commission.

"*White.*—Not so, my lord; my conscience witnesseth otherwise....

"*Dean of Westminster.*—You will not, then, be obedient to the Queen's commands? [70]

'*White.*—I would only avoid those things which have no warrant in the word of God; that are neither decent nor edifying, but are flatly contrary....

"*L. C. J.*—You would have no laws.

"*White.*—If there were no laws, I would live a Christian and do no wrong; if I received any, so it were.

"*L. C. J.*—Thou art a rebel.

"*White.*—Not so, my lord: a true subject.

"*L. C. J.*—Yes, I swear by God, thou art a very rebel; for thou wouldst draw thy sword, and lift up thy hand against thy prince, if time served.

"*White.*—My lord, I thank God my heart standeth right toward *God and my prince; and God will not condemn, though your honor hath so judged.*

"*L. C. J.*—Take him away.

"*White.*—I would speak a word which I am sure will offend, and yet I must speak it; I heard the name of God taken in vain; if I had done it, it had been a greater offense there than that which I stand here for.

"*Mr. Gerard.*—White, White, you don't behave yourself well.

"*White.*—I pray your worship show me wherein, and I will beg pardon and amend it.

"*L. C. J.*—I may swear in a matter of charity....

"*White.*—Pray, my lord, let me have justice. I am unjustly committed; I desire a copy of my presentment.

"*L. C. J.*—You shall have your head from your shoulders. Have him to the Gatehouse.

"*White.*—I pray you to commit me to some prison in London, that I may be near my house.

"*L. C. J.*—No, sir, you shall go thither.

"*White.*—I have paid fines and fees in other prisons; send me not where I shall pay them over again.

"*L. C. J.*—Yes, marry, shall you; this is your glory.

"*White.*—I desire no such glory.

"*L. C. J.*—It will cost you twenty pounds, I warrant you, before you come out.

"*White.*—God's will be done."—*Neal's* "*History of the Puritans*," *Vol. I, chap. V.*

When the Puritans of New England had established their theocracy, they inflicted the same things upon dissenters [71] there that the Government of England had inflicted upon their religious kindred in England. A single scene from their judicial(?) procedure will serve to illustrate the point before us. It is from the condemnation—we do not say the trial—of Mrs. Hutchinson.

Anne Hutchinson was an honorable woman, a Christian. She believed in the abiding presence of the Holy Spirit, according to the word of Christ. She believed also the promise of Christ, that the Spirit will guide the Christian, especially in the understanding of the Scriptures. She accordingly thought that "the Holy Ghost dwells in a justified person," and that it is the duty of Christians to "follow the bidding of the Holy Spirit." And as "there was nothing which the orthodox Puritan so steadfastly abhorred as the anarchical pretense of living by the aid of a supernatural light," she was denounced as "weakening the hands and hearts of the people toward the ministers," and as being "like Roger Williams or worse."

She had said that there was a broad difference between the preaching of Mr. Cotton and that of the rest of the ministers, that they did not preach the covenant of grace as clearly as did Mr. Cotton, and that they were not able ministers of the New Testament. This set all the preachers against her, except Cotton, and as the governmental machinery was but the tool of the preachers, she was condemned and prosecuted.

The court was large. The governor, John Winthrop, was presiding judge and prosecuting attorney, both in one. He upbraided her with having spoken things prejudicial to the honor of the ministers, and other things of like enormity. In her defense she had said that she expected to be delivered out of the hands of the court, and referred to some passages in the book of Daniel.

"*The Governor.*—Daniel was delivered by a miracle. Do you think to be delivered so too? [72]

"*Mrs. H.*—I do here speak it before the Court. I look that the Lord should deliver me by his providence.

"*Deputy Governor.*—I desire Mr. Cotton to tell us whether you do approve of Mrs. Hutchinson's revelations as she hath laid them down.

"*Mr. Cotton.*—I know not whether I understand her; but this I say, If she doth expect a deliverance in a way of providence, then I cannot deny it.

"*Governor.*—I see a marvelous providence of God to bring things to this pass.... God by a providence hath answered our desires, and made her lay open herself and the ground of all these disturbances to be by revelations.

"*All the Court.*—We all consent with you.

"*Gov.*—Ey! it is the most desperate enthusiasm in the world.

"*Mr. Endicott.*—I speak in reference to Mr. Cotton.... Whether do you witness for her or against her?

"*Mr. Cotton.*—This is that I said, sir, and my answer is plain, that if she doth look for deliverance from the hand of God by his providence, and the revelation be ... according to a word [of Scripture], then I cannot deny it.

"*Mr. Endicott.*—You give me satisfaction.

"*Deputy Governor.*—No, no; he gives me none at all.

"*Mr. Cotton.*—I pray, sir, give me leave to express myself. In the sense that she speaks, I dare not bear witness against her.

"*Mr. Nowell.*—I think it a devilish delusion.

"*Governor.*—Of all the revelations that ever I heard of, I never read the like ground laid as is for this. The enthusiasts and Anabaptists had never the like.

"*Mr. Peters.*—I can say the same; ... and I think that is very disputable which our Brother Cotton hath spoken.

"*Governor.*—I am persuaded that the revelation she brings forth is delusion.

"*All the Court* (except two or three).—We all believe it; we all believe it....

"*Governor.*—The Court hath already declared themselves satisfied ... concerning the troublesomeness of her spirit and the danger of her course among us, which is not to be suffered. Therefore if it be the mind of the Court that Mrs. Hutchinson ... shall be banished out of our liberties, [73] and imprisoned till she be sent away, let them hold up their hands.

"All but three responded.

"*Governor.*—Those contrary-minded hold up yours.

"Two only responded.

"*Governor.*—Mrs. Hutchinson, the sentence of the Court you hear is that you are banished from out of our jurisdiction as being a woman not fit for our society, and are to be imprisoned till the Court shall send you away.

"*Mrs. H.*—I desire to know wherefore I am banished.

"*Governor.*—Say no more; the Court knows wherefore, and is satisfied."

"*Emancipation of Massachusetts,*" *pp. 72-75;* "*The Two Republics,*" *pp. 612-618.*

Hitherto it has been supposed by the American people that we had been delivered from such judicial procedure as is represented in these two court scenes, and that citizens of the United States were free from attacks and abuse from the judicial bench on account of their religious beliefs and feelings. But when we are confronted with the fact that from a judicial bench of the United States thousands of citizens of the United States are falsely charged, to their reproach, and denounced as "disingenuous," and branded with the epithet of "fanaticism," solely on account of their "religious feelings," and their *beliefs* and *wishes* with respect to religious observances, then it is certainly time for the people of the United States to look about them, and inquire whether the rights and liberties bequeathed to us by our fathers are indeed all a delusion and a snare.

Of course, this is all consistent with the Judge's views of the relationship of religion and the civil power, and the prerogatives of those religionists who can secure control of legislation, and thus enforce upon all their own religious beliefs and observances. But in this, as in every other point of his *dictum*, the Judge's ideas become a court of the Dark Ages more than any court of the nineteenth century; and a country dominated by papal principles, instead of one dominated [74] by the principles of the Declaration of Independence, and the United States Constitution.

If the jurisdiction of the courts of the United States stands indeed in things religious as well as things civil, and if the judges of those courts really sit in the place of God and enjoy the infallibility that belongs to such position, then it is proper enough, of course, that they should exercise that prerogative in deciding for individuals and sects what their religious beliefs and wishes really are, and whether a religious feeling is fanaticism or not. But if such be not the jurisdiction of the courts nor the position of the judges, then they are entirely out of place when they assume to themselves such jurisdiction and exercise such prerogatives.

And that such is not the jurisdiction of any court of the United States, nor the position of any judge thereof, is evident from every principle of the Declaration of Independence and of the Constitution of the United States, and also from the whole history of the formation of that Constitution.

We may here well cite a passage from a decision of the Supreme Court of California, in a case involving the identical question and principle that was before the Circuit Court of the United States for the Western District of Tennessee. The principles set forth by the California Court are fully as applicable to the United States as they are to that State. We are sure that upon a comparison between this extract and that from Judge Hammond at the beginning of this division, no reader will have the slightest difficulty in deciding which has the true ring, or which sets forth the true American doctrine. The California Court said:—

"The protection of the Constitution extends to every individual or to none. It is the individual that is to be protected. The principle is the same, whether the many or the few are concerned. The Constitution did not mean to inquire how many or how few would profess or not profess this or that particular religion. If there be but a single individual [75] in the State who professes a particular faith, he is as much within the sacred protection of the Constitution as if he agreed with the great majority of his fellow-citizens.

"We cannot, therefore, inquire into the particular views of the petitioner, or any other individual.... The Constitution protects the freedom of religious *profession* and worship, without regard to the sincerity or insincerity of the worshipers. We could not inquire into the fact whether the individual professing to hold a particular day as his Sabbath was sincere or otherwise. He has the right to profess and worship as he pleases, without having his motives inquired into. His motives in exercising a constitutional privilege are matters too sacred for judicial scrutiny. Every citizen has the undoubted right to vote and worship as he pleases, without having his motives impeached in any tribunal of the State."—*Cal. Rep. 9 Lee, 515.*

And let all the people forever say, Amen.

CHAPTER 11

WHAT HAS GOD ENJOINED?

But the Judge does not confine himself, in his exercise of the divine prerogative, merely to deciding for citizens of the United States what they really believe and wish religiously, and that they are disingenuous, and whether their religious feelings are fanaticism or not. He proceeds even to the point of judicially declaring *what God has enjoined*. He reaches this point in the following words:—

"It is not necessary to maintain that to violate the Sunday observance custom [the act] shall be of itself immoral, to make it criminal in the eyes of the law. It may be harmless in itself (because, as petitioner believes, God has not set apart that day for rest and holiness) to work on Sunday; and yet, *if man has set it apart*, in due form, by his law, for rest, *it must be obeyed as man's law if not as God's law*; and it is just as evil to violate such a law, in the eyes of the world, as one sanctioned by God—I mean just as criminal in law.... Or to express it otherwise, there is in one sense [76] a certain immorality in refusing obedience to the laws of one's country, subjection to which *God himself has enjoined upon us.*"

As we are not yet convinced that the Judge has rightfully assumed the prerogative of officially declaring what the will of God is, we desire to know how he knows that God has enjoined subjection to the laws of one's country, in the sense conveyed in this statement and this *dictum* throughout?—that is, that we must be in unqualified subjection to whatever laws men may at any time and in any wise enact, even though they be such laws as may be demanded by "a sort of factitious advantage" of a set of religionists, "in spite of the clamor for religious freedom, and the progress that has been made in the absolute separation of Church and State."

Everybody who has ever read the Bible knows that God has never enjoined subjection to the laws or governments of men in any such sense as that. It is true that the powers which be are ordained of God; but it is also true that these powers are not ordained to act in the place of God. He who has ordained these powers, and set over them "the basest of men" (Daniel 4:17), has also set a limit to their jurisdiction.

Only the things that are Caesar's are to be rendered to Caesar. With anything that pertains to God, government can never have anything to do. The limit of governmental jurisdiction is the citizen's relation to his fellow-citizens or to the State. This jurisdiction is to be exercised in maintaining "civil order and peace." So long as a man conducts himself peaceably and pays his taxes, with him the State can have nothing to do. No State, therefore, can ever of right prohibit anything *which is harmless in itself.* To attempt to do so is the first step toward a despotism.

The Bible *principles* of the limits of State jurisdiction as regards religion, need not here be discussed. God has given *practical examples*, which not only illustrate the principles, but which so flatly and positively contradict the [77] theory propounded by Judge Hammond, that it will be necessary only to note some of them in this connection. Besides, as the Judge has taken upon him to declare for citizens of the United States just what God has enjoined in this respect, it is perfectly in order for us to read for ourselves what, in practice as well as in principle, God has *really* enjoined.

The king of Babylon once set up a great image, and called a grand general assembly of the people to celebrate the dedication of it. On the set day all were commanded to bow down and worship the golden image. There were three Jews who flatly refused. By "a sort of factitious advantage" the worshipers of the image had "the aid of the civil law, and adhered to that advantage with great tenacity, in spite of the clamor for religious freedom." The image-worshipers therefore insisted that these three "non-conformists" should be conformists, as they were "required, every one of them, to comply" with this certain ceremony.

The dissenters refused to comply. By the image-worshipers this refusal was held to be a defiant setting up of the dissenters' "non-observance by an ostentatious display of their disrespect for the feelings or prejudices of others." And as the dissenters were held to be "ostentatiously" refusing "for the purpose of emphasizing their distaste for or their disbelief in the custom" of image-worship, they were "made to suffer for their defiance by persecutions, if you call them so, on the part of the great majority" of image-worshipers, who would compel them to worship when *they* worshiped.

The penalty of the law was that whoever should refuse to worship the image, should be cast into a burning fiery furnace. As the image-worshipers were very tenacious of their "sort of factitious advantage," they prosecuted the three non-conformists. And what made the image-worshipers yet more tenacious of their "sort of factitious advantage," was [78] the fact that the dissenters not only refused to conform, but maintained the inalienable right to dissent from every phase of the proposed custom.

When prosecuted, the non-conformists in open court refused to conform, and asserted their right to refuse. The judge declared to them distinctly the alternative, "If ... ye fall down and worship the image, ... well; but if ye worship not, ye shall be cast the same hour into the midst of a burning fiery furnace; and who is that God that shall deliver you out of my hands?"

The three non-conformists replied to the judge, "We are not careful to answer thee in this matter. If it be so, our God whom we serve is able to deliver us from the burning fiery furnace, and he will deliver us out of thine hand.... But if not, be it known unto thee ... that we will not serve thy gods, nor worship the golden image which thou hast set up."

The judge was naturally inclined to favor the image-worshipers, and as public opinion was clearly on their side, too, he was not willing to admit that the prisoners could "shelter themselves just yet behind the doctrines of religious freedom in defying the existence of a law and its application to them which was distasteful to their own religious feeling or fanaticism," that it was their right to worship according to the dictates of their own consciences. He held that as the law had commanded "in due form" the observance of this rite, "it must be obeyed as man's law if not as God's law." This, too, the more especially, as the Lord had plainly told them to "serve the king of Babylon, and live;" and to "seek the peace of the city whither they had been carried away captive." Jeremiah 26:17; 29:7.

It is true the thing which the dissenters were doing was "harmless in itself," but that could not be allowed any weight, because the law commanded it, and therefore it was held that there was a "certain immorality in refusing obedience [79] to the laws of one's country, subjection to which God himself had enjoined." Therefore, "full of fury" and with "the form of his visage changed," the judge commanded that the furnace should be heated seven times hotter than usual, and that the prisoners should be "remanded" to its fiery embraces.

The judge was the king himself, and no sooner was his judgment executed, and the men cast into the flames, than he was more astonished than ever before in his life. He "rose up in haste, and spake, and said unto his counselors, Did not we cast three men bound into the midst of the fire? They answered, and said unto the king, True, O king. He answered and said, Lo, I see *four* men *loose*, walking in the midst of the fire, and they have no hurt; and the form of the fourth is like the Son of God." Then the king called to the non-conformists, "Ye servants of the most high God, come forth, and come hither."

The king had learned something. He spake and said: "Blessed be the God of Shadrach, Meshach, and Abednego, who hath sent his angel, and delivered his servants that trusted in him, *and have changed the king's word*, and yielded their bodies, *that they might not serve* nor *worship* any god except their own God."

The king had learned that God had not enjoined subjection to the laws of the country in anything that pertained to the rights of the individual to worship. He had learned that when the laws of the country prohibit that which is harmless in itself, and thus interfere with the right of the individual to enjoy his God-given rights, then it is the law that is wrong, and not the action of the person who disregards the law; and that therefore the proper thing to do is to *change the law*, not to punish the harmless individual.

Yes, King Nebuchadnezzar, heathen though he was, learned that much nearly twenty-five hundred years ago. And when the Declaration of Independence and the Constitutions of [80] the United States and of the several States, have embodied for this whole nation this same doctrine, in the words, "All men are created equal, and are endowed by their Creator with certain unalienable rights, among which are life, liberty, and the pursuit of happiness," and, "No human power can *in any case whatever* control or interfere with the rights of conscience," it is scarcely to the credit of a judge of a court of the United States that he should be further behind the times than was the heathen Nebuchadnezzar nearly twenty-five hundred years ago.

Nor is this the only example in illustration of the principle. About sixty-five years later, in the reign of Darius the Mede, some arrogant religionists again, by "a sort of factitious advantage, secured the aid of the civil law." Consequently, again a thing harmless in itself was forbidden by law, and man's law presumed to dictate as to when and how men should worship. There was a single non-conformist who again "ostentatiously displayed his distaste for and his disbelief in the custom" sought to be enforced by law. He too was made to suffer for his defiance, "by persecutions on the part of the great majority." He was cast into a den of lions. But the next morning he was able to announce, "*My God hath sent his angel*, and hath shut the lions' mouths, that they have not hurt me; *forasmuch as before him innocency was found in me*; and also before thee, O king, *have I done no hurt.*"

Again God declared the man innocent who disregards any law touching religious exercises, or prohibiting in such connection that which is harmless in itself. Again God demonstrated that he has not enjoined subjection to the laws of one's country in any such things as these, or in any such sense as this.

About five hundred and sixty years afterward occurred another example illustrating the same thing. Some religionists, by "a sort of factitious advantage," had the aid of the [81] civil law, and "adhered to that advantage with great tenacity, in spite of the great clamor for religious freedom." "Then the high-priest rose up, and all they that were with him, ... and were filled with indignation, and laid their hands on the apostles, and put them in the common prison. *But the angel of the Lord* by night *opened the prison doors, and brought them forth, and said,* Go, stand and speak in the temple to the people all the words of this life." Acts 5:17-20.

Thus again it is shown, not only that God never enjoined any such thing as Judge Hammond says he has, in the sense there argued, but that he has positively enjoined the opposite. In short, by these evidences, and volumes more that might be produced, it is demonstrated that the Judge's assumption of the prerogative of officially declaring what God has enjoined, is about as wide of the mark as is his like attempt authoritatively to declare what the "religious feelings," "beliefs, and wishes" of the Seventh-day Adventists "really" are.

But the strangest and most incongruous thing about the whole procedure is that a judge of any court in the United States should presume to do it at all.

CHAPTER 12

THE RIGHTS OF THE PEOPLE

In our study of this opinion we have found that in the whole *dictum* there is nowhere any recognition whatever of any such thing as the rights of the individual conscience, nor any right of the individual to choose for himself in religion or religious observances. Everything must be submitted to the dictates of the majority, it matters not what that majority may declare or demand. In short, the will of the majority is made absolute in all things. The State is made supreme [82] and absolute, and the individual is completely swallowed up and absorbed therein. The majority alone have rights, and these are bestowed by the State.

This point was merely referred to in the quotation last made above. It is worthy of fuller examination, therefore we quote:—

"The crime is in doing the thing forbidden by law, harmless though it be in itself. Therefore, all that part of the argument that it is not hurtful in itself to work on Sunday, apart from the religious sanctity of the day, is beside the question; for it may be that the courts would hold that repeated repetitions of a violation of law forbidding even a harmless thing, could be a nuisance as tending to a breach of the peace.... That is to say, a nuisance might be predicated of an act harmless in itself, if the will of the majority had lawfully forbidden the act, and rebellion against that will would be the *gravamen* of the offense."

Now in view of this statement, please read carefully the following:—

"We hold these truths to be self-evident, that all men are created equal; that they are endowed by their Creator with certain *unalienable rights*; that *among these* are life, liberty, *and the pursuit of happiness*. That *to secure these rights*, governments are instituted among men, deriving their just powers from the consent of the governed; that whenever any form of government becomes destructive of these ends, it is *the right of the people* to alter or abolish it, and to institute a new government, laying its foundation on such principles, and organizing its powers in such form, as *to them* shall seem most likely to effect their safety and happiness."

In declaring that governments derive their just powers from the consent of the governed, there is declared not only the *sovereignty* of the people, but the entire *capability* of the people. And in declaring the equal and inalienable right of all men to life, liberty, and the pursuit of happiness, there is declared the entire capability of every man to enjoy life and liberty, and to pursue happiness, *as he may think best*, and *as [83] he may choose for himself*, so long as he *interferes with no other man's equal right* to the enjoyment of life, liberty, and the pursuit of happiness. This is the only limit that ever can rightly be set to the exercise of this right, and this limit is set in the very Declaration itself. Indeed, the Declaration itself presupposes that men are men indeed, and that as such they are fully capable of deciding for themselves as to what is best for their happiness, and how they shall pursue it.

No man can ever interfere with any other person's right to the enjoyment of life, liberty, and the pursuit of happiness, by doing that which is harmless in itself. Therefore no government, no law, can ever of right forbid the doing of anything that is harmless in itself.

Governments are not formed to interfere with or to restrict inalienable rights; but to *secure*, to guard, to make firm, the enjoyment thereof. These rights men already possess as men, by virtue of being men in society, and not by virtue of government. These rights were theirs before government was; they were *their own* in the essential meaning of the term. These rights men "do not hold, by any subinfeudation, but by direct homage and allegiance to the owner and Lord of all",[1]—their Creator, who has endowed them with these rights.

It is not the prerogative, because it is not the purpose, of government to put any restriction, limitation, or qualification upon these rights, but solely to *secure* them.

"For the rights of man, as man, must be understood in a sense that can admit of no single exception; for to allege an exception is the same thing as to deny the principle. We reject, therefore, with scorn, any profession of respect to the principle, which, in fact, comes to us clogged and contradicted by a petition for an exception.... To profess the principle and then to plead for an exception, let the plea be what it may, is to deny the principle; and it

---

[1] Stanley Matthews.

is to utter a treason against humanity. The rights of man must everywhere [84] all the world over, be recognized and respected."—*Isaac Taylor.* [2]

The plea that the doing of a harmless thing, or even the repetition of it to an infinite extent, could ever tend to a breach of the peace, is most puerile, and is as despotic as it is puerile. The idea is this: You are going quietly on your way, doing something which is harmless in itself. But I see you, and I am of so splenetic, irritable, and despotic a disposition, that out of sheer wickedness I attack you. A breach of the peace has been committed; but lo, instead of punishing me for the breach of the peace, a law must be enacted *forbidding you ever again to do that harmless thing*! And this, forsooth, because it tends to a breach of the peace! You must submit to be robbed of your inalienable right, and be compelled to surrender it a tribute to the overbearing demands of my tyrannical disposition. The innocent citizen must be made a slave, and the tyrannical meddler must be clothed with power! In such a conception there is no recognition of any such thing as an inalienable right. Such an idea is the very essence of despotism. Such a government would be an unmitigated tyranny.

Therefore, let it be forever repeated, that no law can ever justly be made forbidding the doing of anything that is harmless in itself. Such a law is wrong and essentially tyrannical in itself. Such a *law* is not simply an *utterance*, but an *enactment*, of a treason against humanity. And it is no less so when formulated by judicial or parliamentary legislation than by the arbitrary decree of a despot. Such ideas of law and government have no place under the Declaration of Independence or the United States Constitution.

The jurisdiction of the State and United States Governments— [85] "Is both derivative and limited. It is limited with regard to the co-ordinate departments; more necessarily is it limited with regard to the constituents. The preservation of a free government required not merely that the metes and bounds which separate each department of power be invariably maintained, but more especially that neither of them be suffered *to overleap the great barrier which defends the rights of the people.* The rulers who are guilty of such an encroachment, exceed the commission from which they derive their authority, and are tyrants. The people who submit to it are governed by laws made neither by themselves nor by any authority derived from them, and are slaves."—*James Madison.*

---

[2] Quoted by Stanley Matthews in the Case of Cincinnati School Board on Bible in the Public Schools.

The truth, and the *sum* of this whole discussion, is that the views propounded in the *dictum* of Judge Hammond in the King case, are all the way from one hundred to nineteen hundred years behind the times; they are as though history had never been written; they are a parody upon progress, a travesty upon justice, and are subversive of every principle of the Declaration of Independence and the United States Constitution. They would sweep away every right, either civil or religious, that is declared or secured by the Declaration and the Constitution, and would again establish the same old despotism, both civil and religious, which cursed the world for seventeen hundred years, and against which the Declaration and the Constitution are, and were intended to be, an everlasting protest.

CHAPTER 13

⟶»⟶ ❖❖❖ ⟵«⟵

THE LOGIC OF THE
JUDGE'S POSITION

In an unofficial communication of later date than his *dictum* in this case, Judge Hammond has gone over the same ground again, and has made some additional statements, which are of interest as well as of importance in connection with the statements which we have already noticed. [86]

After reiterating one of the main propositions of the *dictum*,—that "the institution of Sunday, like the religion upon which it is founded, belongs to the people as a characteristic possession," that therefore religion is essentially a part of the laws, and its preservation as such "a necessity of statesmanship,"—he makes the following important admission:—

> "*The logic of this position may lead to a union of Church and State, undoubtedly*; but it is not essential nor always useful, indeed often otherwise, to go to the end of one's logic."

In this review we have demonstrated again and again, from his own propositions, that a union of Church and State is logically inherent in the positions assumed throughout that document. It is well, therefore, for our readers to know that he sees and acknowledges the same thing himself. And from this it is perfectly proper, as well as logical, to inquire, Is it the province of a judge of a United States Court to inculcate from his official seat the doctrine of a union of Church and State in these United States? At his induction into that responsible office he took a solemn oath to support the Constitution of the United States, which, both in its principles and its specific precepts, is diametrically opposed to a union of Church and State, and to every position the logic of which would lead to a union of Church and State.

His plea, that it is not essential to go to the end of one's logic, is as puerile as is his other position that government may prohibit a thing harmless in itself to prevent "breach of the peace." It is a pitiable thing indeed when a person insists upon maintaining a position, the logic of which he is unwilling to follow to its legitimate end. But this is not all there is in this case. It would be bad enough were this so only with him as an individual. But this is not so. He occupies the place of a judge of the United States, a representative [87] of the judicial department of the Government of the United States. As such he has spoken; as such he has taken this position; and as such he has given to the position, as far as in him lies, the weight of the authority of the high office which he holds. And just as certainly as the position which he has taken should be confirmed by the higher court as the position of the Government, just so certainly it would be entirely and forever beyond his power either to check or to control the logic of it in any way; and just so certainly would the religious element that is enlisted and favored in this thing, see that the logic of the position was carried fully to the end which even he sees and acknowledges is involved in it.

The truth is that government is one of the most intensely logical things in this world. A position taken to-day may not reach the end of its logic in a generation, or in two generations, or even in a hundred years. But if it be a position involving an important principle such as this, it *will* reach the end of its logic as certainly as the government continues.

Yet Judge Hammond, not content with such a display of logical acumen as the above, and as though to annihilate all basis for any logical deduction of any kind whatever, proceeds to lay down as "the truth" this astounding proposition:—

"The truth is that no principle or dogma of government, or of any other human conduct, can be applied according to the inexorable tendency of its logic."

Briefly stated, this says that no principle of human conduct can be logically applied. But it is difficult to conceive how any person, who ever drew a single conclusion in his life and acted upon it, could soberly make such a statement. It is true that some men in some things are erratic, inconsistent, illogical. But all history demonstrates in a thousand ways that with humanity, whether viewed in the individual or [88] in government, principles of human conduct are applied strictly according to the inexorable tendency of their logic. Indeed, it would be an easy task to develop the principle of human conduct, the inexorable tendency of the logic of which has produced this very *dictum* upon which we have been required to bestow so much attention.

As a matter of fact, to admit the truth of the proposition here quoted would be to renounce the very faculty of reason or intelligence itself; which, by the way, is but the inexorable tendency of the logic of Judge Hammond's position.

Another important statement in emphasis of positions taken in the *dictum* is the following:—

> "It is a somewhat humiliating spectacle to see the Sunday advocates trying to justify the continuance of Sunday legislation ... upon the argument that it is not in conflict with the civic dogma of religious freedom. *It surely is.*"

Yet in the face of every constitutional provision, State and national, touching the question, he persists in justifying this palpable conflict with the civic dogma of religious freedom, by still arguing that—

> "The bare fact that the mass desires Sunday as the public day of rest, is enough to justify its civic sanction; and the potentiality of *the fact that it is in aid of the religion* of that mass *might be frankly confessed and not denied.*"

This is again but to justify every piece of religious persecution that was ever inflicted in this world. And under such dogma as this, all that is required for this whole line of enforced religious observances and persecutions to be taken up and carried forward again, is that "the mass" shall demand it. And so far as Judge Hammond's jurisdiction could be made to extend, the whole power of the Government, whether State or national, would be exerted in behalf of this mass, who should choose to pursue a course "in conflict with the civic dogma of religious freedom." In view of these statements we should like to have the Judge explain just what is the civic dogma of religious freedom. [89]

Yet further, and in his very last words, so far, on the subject, he still justifies the doctrine of persecution in the following sentence:—

> "It is also noticeable that the early Christians commenced their assaults upon the old religions by a disregard of their holy days, and for this they were first persecuted by the law, as they [*sic*] now persecute therewith the Jews and the Seventh-day Adventists."

We are not by any means ready to admit that it is the early Christians who *now* persecute the Jews and the Seventh-day Adventists. Neither the early Christians nor any other Christians, either now or at any other time, ever did persecute. If any man persecutes, he is not a Christian. It is true that the early Christians were persecuted, by "due process of law," too, precisely as the Jews and the Seventh-day Adventists are now persecuted by "due process of law." The persecution then was heathenish, and so it is now. The "due process of law" by which the persecution was then legalized and justified, was but the manifestation of the "inexorable tendency of the logic" of the pagan "principle of human conduct," and such only it is now.

And with the persecuted Jews and Seventh-day Adventists we are only glad to stand and be classed with the early Christians, to bear their reproach and to share their sufferings; as we know that in suffering with them we are suffering with Him with whom they suffered. And "it is a faithful saying, If we suffer with him, we shall also reign with him." And he is the Author of a religious liberty which is absolute and eternal. [90]

CHAPTER 14

WHENCE CAME IT ALL?

From the extracts which we have made and discussed in this review, we have no doubt that the reader has wondered where in the world a judge of a United States Court ever could have got such an abundance of such strange principles. He was sitting in the place, and speaking officially from the bench, of a judge of a court of the Government of the United States. It were to be expected, therefore, that he would announce the principles of that Government. Instead of this, however, he boldly sets forth propositions and principles that are utterly subversive of every principle of the Government of the United States, as that Government was originally established, and as the people have supposed it was being maintained.

Where did he get them? We are not left to answer this question ourselves, nor in a way in which there need be any fear of making a mistake. The answer is already and abundantly made, and furnished ready to our hand. All we need to do is to transcribe such portions as may be required to answer the inquiry that has been raised.

The decision of the court and the *dictum* of the Judge were filed at Memphis, Tennessee, Aug. 1, 1891, and were printed in full in the Memphis *Appeal-Avalanche* of the next day, August 2. Then in the same paper, under date of August 30, there is a communication nearly four columns in length, entitled, "The Sunday Habit," upon the same subject, covering the same ground, signed "E. S. Hammond," and dated "Aug. 12, 1891." The head-lines of the communication show that the E. S. Hammond whose name is signed to it is the same one, who, as Judge E. S. Hammond, filed the *dictum* August 1, which was printed August 2. And every line of the communication plainly shows that it was from *Mr.* E. S. Hammond, *the individual*, that *Hon.* E. S. Hammond [91] *the judge*, obtained the principles and propositions which are set forth in the *dictum*.

Nor were they simply gotten up for the occasion, or prepared on short notice. By *Mr.* Hammond's express statement they are shown to have been of long standing, if not inherent in the individual. After stating again some of the leading thoughts of the *dictum* of the judge, Mr. Hammond, with a satisfaction that is clearly apparent, announces that:—

> "Upon this line of argument, the writer *some years ago*, being invited to lecture before his Jewish fellow-citizens upon the question whether Christianity can be a part of the law of the land, sought to reconcile them to the civic doctrine of obedience to a dominant though distasteful custom, even at the economic sacrifice of another day of labor, rather than attempt to overthrow a habit so fixed as the Sunday habit, by the comparatively weak process of individual defiance of the custom, and to agitate the incorporation of an exception in the Sunday laws in favor of him who conscientiously had abstained from labor on Saturday."

This shows that the doctrine of obedience to a dominant religious party, which, by "a sort of factitious advantage" may control the civil power, and by it compel conformity to their religious opinions or dogmas, is an old and favorite doctrine of Mr. Hammond's. And he seems to be so smitten with his despotic principles that he not only seizes every opportunity to air them and parade them before the public, but must needs use the judicial office of the United States to create an opportunity.

As for his effort to reconcile his Jewish fellow-citizens to his doctrine, we can say: First, unless his Jewish fellow-citizens of Tennessee are much more financially liberal than they are in any other part of the country, they would hardly appreciate his request that they pay sixteen and two thirds per cent of their income for the privilege of being reconciled to "the civic doctrine" of obedience to a dominant and distasteful religious custom; and, secondly and above all, unless they [92] are entirely lost to the religious integrity that has always characterized their race, they would still less appreciate his invitation to surrender to a dominant party and to a distasteful custom, all their rights of conscience, for the privilege of being so reconciled.

For to surrender all their rights of conscience is just what he asks them to do. For when an exception is either asked or granted, upon the condition that those who are excepted shall "conscientiously" abstain from labor on another day, it then becomes a matter of judicial decision as to what is conscientious abstinence or observance. This has already been declared by the courts of those States which have exemption clauses in their Sunday laws. The decisions have declared that the burden of proof of conscientious action rests upon him who makes the claim of exception on account of conscientious observance of another day, and the proof must be such *as will satisfy the court.*

Thus it is demonstrated that Mr. Hammond's proposition, of which he seems to be so proud, is simply a proposal that citizens of the United States and of the State of Tennessee shall surrender to the control of courts and juries their conscientious convictions, their conscientious beliefs, and their conscientious observances; that they shall no longer observe the Sabbath according to the dictates of their own consciences, but only according to the dictates *of the courts.*

This is precisely the doctrine of the *dictum* of Judge Hammond, and it is evident that it was derived from Mr. E. S. Hammond, *the individual;* for it is in open contradiction to both the Constitution of the United States and of the State of Tennessee, both of which were specifically before the Judge when he set forth his *dictum.*

The Constitution of the State of Tennessee, whose citizens Mr. Hammond was endeavoring to reconcile to the dictates of a dominant religious party, by asking them to surrender to the courts their rights of conscience, plainly [93] declares that "no human authority can *in any case whatever* control or interfere with the rights of conscience." Therefore it is plain that in the proposal which Mr. Hammond made to his Jewish fellow-citizens of Tennessee, he spoke in open contradiction to the Constitution of that State, as well as in total oblivion of every principle of the rights of conscience; and actually advised his Jewish fellow-citizens to surrender their explicitly declared Constitutional rights, as well as their own individual and divine rights of conscience.

The Constitution of the United States, which Judge Hammond is empowered to construe, which he is sworn faithfully to maintain, and which is intended to be the supreme guide in all the deliverances which he renders from the bench upon which he sits—"the American Constitution, in harmony with the people of the several States—withholds from the Federal Government the power *to invade* the home of reason, *the citadel of conscience.*" It is evident, therefore, that the principles of that *dictum* were not derived in any sense from the Constitution which the Judge is sworn to maintain, and which is intended to be his guide; nor were they derived from the Constitution of Tennessee, which at the time was subject to his cognizance.

Therefore, as the principles of Judge Hammond's *dictum* are *not* the principles of either the Constitution of the United States or of the State of Tennessee, both of which were the direct subject of his judicial cognizance; and as they are explicitly the principles of Mr. E. S. Hammond, *the individual*, as expressed in his communication of Aug. 12, 1891, to the *Appeal-Avalanche*, and set forth "some years ago" from the lecture platform, it logically follows that the principles announced in the *dictum* of Hon. E. S. Hammond, *the judge*, were derived solely from Mr. E. S. Hammond, *the individual*. And from this it follows inevitably that upon the question of religious right, Hon. E. S. Hammond, of the Circuit Court of the United States, has not hesitated to set forth, from the [94] judicial bench of the United States, his own personal and individual opinions, to clothe them as far as possible with the authority that attaches to such a position, and to pass them off upon the American people as the principles of the Government of the United States.

This illustrates another point, and one which all history emphasizes: that is, that whenever religion becomes in any way connected with the civil power, it is always *the personal opinions* as to religion, of those who happen at the time to be in power, that are given the force of law which all are expected to accept, and to which all are obliged by authority of Government to submit. And the first essay of the kind by a court of the United States ought to be enough to awaken the people of this nation to the wisdom of the Constitution and of the governmental fathers who made it, in straitly forbidding the Government to take cognizance of religious things in any way whatever.

Mr. Hammond presumes to announce for the Jews, that which of course he declares to be to their "credit," that "they adopt this [his] plan of compliance." But we are very happy to know and to publish that he also announces that the "Anglo-Saxon who follows the tenet of the Jews as to the Sabbath, is more irreconcilable to the sacrifice he is called to make."

All honor to such Anglo-Saxons then! May their tribe increase abundantly! And we sincerely hope that every one of them will forever remain completely irreconcilable to any such sacrifice or compliance. Better a thousand times to die as poor King, the victim in this case, did, condemned by such "process of law" and under a $1,000 bail, or even in a dungeon, than to comply with the bigoted demands of a religious party, who, "in spite of the clamor for religious freedom and the progress that has been made in the absolute separation of Church and State," and by "a sort of factitious advantage," "have secured the aid of the civil law!" [95] Better to die the freemen of Jesus Christ, than to live the slaves of a religious despotism!

R. M. King, the victim of this persecution, is dead. He died as he had lived, a humble, harmless man, and a sincere Christian. He died condemned by the courts of Tennessee and the Circuit Court of the United States, and bound in $1,000 bail on appeal to the Supreme Court of the United States. By his death his case has passed from earthly courts, and stands appealed to the Supreme Court of the Universe.

That Court will surely sit, for God "hath appointed a day in the which he will judge the world in righteousness." In that day there will sit a Judge with whom neither "factitious advantage" nor "public opinion," but only *justice*, shall have any weight. And in that day we would far rather stand in Mr. King's place than in that of his persecutors; for He who shall sit as Judge in that day, has long ago declared, "Inasmuch as ye have done it unto one of the least of these my brethren, ye have done it unto me;" and, "Whoso shall offend one of these little ones which believe in me, it were better for him that a millstone were hanged about his neck, and that he were drowned in the depth of the sea."

APPENDIX

Supreme Court of California, Ex-Parte Newman

By special request we reprint here the decision of the California Supreme Court, from which we have several times quoted in this review. It is well worthy of universal circulation and acceptance, as it is the only judicial decision ever rendered upon the question of Sunday observance that accords with the common principles of right or justice, with American principles as announced in the Declaration of Independence and the national and State Constitutions, or with Christian principles. Would that the principles of this masterly decision might become ingrained in the intellectual make-up of every person in the United States:—

Terry, C. J.—The petitioner was tried and convicted before a justice of the peace for a violation of the Act of April, 1858, entitled, "An Act for the Better Observance of the Sabbath," and upon his failure to pay the fine imposed, was imprisoned.

The counsel for petitioner moves his discharge, on the ground that the Act under which these proceedings were had is in conflict with the first and fourth sections of the first Article of the State Constitution, and therefore void.

The first section declares, "All men are by nature free and independent, and have certain inalienable rights, among which are those of enjoying and defending life and liberty; acquiring, possessing, and protecting property; and pursuing and obtaining safety and happiness."

The fourth section declares, "The free exercise and enjoyment of religious profession and worship, without discrimination or preference, shall forever be allowed in this State."

The questions which arise in the consideration of the case, are:—

1. Does the act of the Legislature make a discrimination or preference favorable to one religious profession? or is it a mere civil rule of conduct? [96-98]

2. Has the Legislature the power to enact a municipal regulation which enforces upon the citizen a compulsory abstinence from his ordinary lawful and peaceable avocations for one day in the week?

There is no expression in the Act under consideration which can lead to the conclusion that it was intended as a civil rule, as contradistinguished from a law for the benefit of religion. It is entitled, "An Act for the Better Observance of the Sabbath," and the prohibitions in the body of the Act are confined to the "Christian Sabbath."

It is, however, contended, on the authority of some of the decisions of other States, that notwithstanding the pointed language of the Act, it may be construed into a civil rule of action, and that the result would be the same, even if the language were essentially different.

The fault of this argument is that it is opposed to the universally admitted rule which requires a law to be construed according to the intention of the law-maker, and this intention to be gathered from the language of the law, according to its plain and common acceptation.

It is contended that a civil rule requiring the devotion of one seventh of the time to repose is an absolute necessity, and the want of it has been dilated upon as a great evil to society. But have the Legislature so considered it? Such an assumption is not warranted by anything contained in the Sunday law. On the contrary, the intention which pervades the whole Act is to enforce, as a religious institution, the observance of a day held sacred by the followers of one faith, and entirely disregarded by all the other denominations within the State. The whole scope of the Act is expressive of an intention on the part of the Legislature to require a periodical cessation from ordinary pursuits, not as a civil duty necessary for the repression of any existing evil, but in furtherance of the interests, and in aid of the devotions, of those who profess the Christian religion.

Several authorities, affirming the validity of similar statutes, have been cited from the reports of other States. While we entertain a profound respect for the courts of our sister States, we do not feel called upon to yield our convictions of right to a blind adherence to precedent; especially when they are, in our opinion, opposed to principle; and the reasoning by which they are endeavored to be supported is by no means satisfactory or convincing. In Bryan *vs.* Berry (6 Cal. 398), in reference to the decisions of other States, we said: "Decided cases are, in some sense, evidence of what the law is. We say in some sense, because it is not so much the decision as it is the reasoning upon which the decision is based, which makes it authority, and requires it to be respected."

It will be unnecessary to examine all the cases cited by the district attorney. The leading cases in which the question is more elaborately discussed than in the others, are the cases of Specht *vs.* the Commonwealth (8 Barr, 313), and the City Council *vs.* Benjamin (2 Strob. 508), decided respectively by the Supreme Courts of Pennsylvania and South Carolina. [99] These decisions are based upon the ground that the statutes requiring the observance of the Christian Sabbath established merely a civil rule, and make no discrimination or preference in favor of any religion. By an examination of these cases, it will be seen that the position taken rests in mere assertion, and that not a single argument is adduced to prove that a preference in favor of the Christian religion is not given by the law. In the case in 8 Barr, the Court said: "It [the law] intermeddles not with the natural and indefeasible right of all men to worship Almighty God according to the dictates of their own consciences; it compels none to attend, erect, or support any place of worship, or to maintain any ministry, against his consent; it pretends not to control or interfere with the rights of conscience, and it establishes no preference for any religious establishment or mode of worship."

This is the substance of the arguments to show that these laws establish no preference. The last clause in the extract asserts the proposition broadly; but it is surely no legitimate conclusion from what precedes it, and must be taken as the plainest example of *petitio principii.* That which precedes it establishes that the law does not destroy religious toleration, but that is all.

Now, does our Constitution, when it forbids discrimination or preference in religion, mean merely to guarantee toleration? For that, in effect, is all which the cases cited seem to award, as the right of a citizen. In a community composed of persons of various religious denominations, having different days of worship, each considering his own as sacred from secular employment, all being equally considered and protected under the Constitution, a law is passed which in effect recognizes the sacred character of one of these days, by compelling all others to abstain from secular employment, which is precisely one of the modes in which its observance is manifested and required by the creed of that sect to which it belongs as a Sabbath. Is not this a discrimination in favor of the one? Does it require more than an appeal to one's common sense to decide that this is a preference? And when the Jew or seventh-day Christian complains of this, is it any answer to say, Your conscience is not constrained, you are not compelled to worship or to perform religious rites on that day, nor forbidden to keep holy the day which you esteem as a Sabbath? We think not, however high the authority which decides otherwise.

When our liberties were acquired, our republican form of government adopted, and our Constitution framed, we deemed that we had attained not only toleration, but religious liberty in its largest sense,—a complete separation between Church and State, and a perfect equality without distinction between all religious sects. "Our Government," says Mr. Johnson, in his celebrated Sunday-mail report, "is a civil and not a religious institution; whatever may be the religious sentiments of citizens, and however variant, they are alike entitled to protection from the Government, so long as they do [100] not invade the rights of others." And again, dwelling upon the danger of applying the powers of government to the furtherance and support of sectarian objects, he remarks, in language which should not be forgotten, but which ought to be deeply impressed on the minds of all who desire to maintain the supremacy of our republican system: "Extensive religious combinations to effect a political object, are, in the opinion of the committee, always dangerous. The first effort of the kind calls for the establishment of a principle which would lay the foundation for dangerous innovation upon the spirit of the Constitution, and upon the religious rights of the citizen. If admitted, it may be justly apprehended that the future measures of the Government will be strangely marked, if not eventually controlled, by the same influence. All religious despotism commences by combination and influence; and when that influence begins to operate upon the political institutions of a country, the civil power soon bends under it, and the catastrophe of other nations furnishes an awful warning of the consequences.... What other nations call religious toleration, we call religious rights; they were not exercised in virtue of governmental indulgence, but as rights of which the Government cannot deprive any portion of her citizens, however small. Despotic power may invade those rights, but justice still confirms them. Let the national Legislature once perform an act which involves the decision of a religious controversy, and it will have passed its legitimate bounds. The precedent will then be established, and the foundation laid for that usurpation of the divine prerogative in this country, which has been the desolating scourge of the fairest portions of the Old World. Our Constitution recognizes no other power than that of persuasion for enforcing religious observances."

We come next to the question whether, considering the Sunday law as a civil regulation, it is in the power of the Legislature to enforce a compulsory abstinence from lawful and ordinary occupation for a given period of time, without some apparent civil necessity for such action; whether a pursuit, which is not only peaceable and lawful, but also praiseworthy and commendable for six days in the week, can be arbitrarily converted into a penal offense or misdemeanor on the seventh. As a general rule, it will be admitted that men have a natural right to do anything which their inclinations may suggest, if it be not evil in itself, and in no way impairs the rights of others. When societies are formed, each individual surrenders certain rights, and as an equivalent for that surrender has secured to him the enjoyment of certain others, appertaining to his person and property, without the protection of which society cannot exist. All legislation is a restraint on individuals, but it is a restraint which must be submitted to by all who would enjoy the benefits derived from the institutions of society.

It is necessary, for the preservation of free institutions, that there should be some general and easily recognized rule, to determine the extent of governmental power, and establish a proper line of demarkation between [101] such as are strictly legitimate and such as are usurpations which invade the reserved rights of the citizen, and infringe upon his constitutional liberty. The true rule of distinction would seem to be that which allows to the Legislature the right so to restrain each one in his freedom of conduct, as to secure perfect protection to all others from every species of danger to person, health, and property; that each individual shall be required so to use his own as not to inflict injury upon his neighbor; and these, we think, are all the immunities which can be justly claimed by one portion of society from another, under a government of constitutional limitation. For these reasons the law restrains the establishment of tanneries, slaughter-houses, gunpowder depots, the discharge of fire-arms, etc., in a city, the sale of drugs and poisons, and the practice of physic by incompetent persons, and makes a variety of other prohibitions, the reason and sense of which are obvious to the most common understanding.

Now, when we come to inquire what reason can be given for the claim of power to enact a Sunday law, we are told, looking at it in its purely civil aspect, that it is absolutely necessary for the benefit of his health and the restoration of his powers; and in aid of this great social necessity, the Legislature may, for the general convenience, set apart a particular day of rest, and require its observance by all.

This argument is founded on the assumption that mankind are in the habit of working too much, and thereby entailing evil upon society; and that, without compulsion, they will not seek the necessary repose which their exhausted natures demand. This is to us a new theory, and is contradicted by the history of the past and the observations of the present. We have heard, in all ages, of declamations and reproaches against the vice of indolence; but we have yet to learn that there has ever been any general complaint of an intemperate, vicious, unhealthy, or morbid industry. On the contrary, we know that mankind seek cessation from toil from the natural influences of self-preservation, in the same manner and as certainly as they seek slumber, relief from pain, or food to appease their hunger.

Again, it may be well considered that the amount of rest which would be required by one half of society may be widely disproportionate to that required by the other. It is a matter of which each individual must be permitted to judge for himself, according to his own instincts and necessities. As well might the Legislature fix the days and hours for work, and enforce their observance by an unbending rule which shall be visited alike upon the weak and strong. Whenever such attempts are made, the law-making power leaves its legitimate sphere, and makes an incursion into the realms of physiology; and its enactments, like the sumptuary laws of the ancients, which prescribe the mode and texture of people's clothing, or similar laws which might prescribe and limit our food and drink, must be regarded as an invasion, without reason or necessity, of the natural rights of the citizen, which are guaranteed by the fundamental law. [102]

The truth is, however much it may be disguised, that this one day of rest is a purely religious idea. Derived from the Sabbatical institutions of the ancient Hebrew, it has been adopted into all the creeds of succeeding religious sects throughout the civilized world; and whether it be the Friday of the Mohammedan, the Saturday of the Israelite, or the Sunday of the Christian, it is alike fixed in the affections of its followers beyond the power of eradication; and in most of the States of our Confederacy, the aid of the law to enforce its observance has been given, under the pretense of a civil, municipal, or police regulation.

But it has been argued that this is a question exclusively for the Legislature; that the law-making power alone has the right to judge of the necessity and character of all police rules, and that there is no power in the judiciary to interfere with the exercise of this right.

One of the objects for which the judicial department is established is the protection of the constitutional rights of the citizen. The question presented in this case is not merely one of expediency or abuse of power; it is a question of usurpation of power. If the Legislature have the authority to appoint a time of compulsory rest, we would have no right to interfere with it, even if they required a cessation from toil for six days in the week instead of one. If they possess this power, it is without limit, and may extend to the prohibition of all occupations at all times.

While we concede to the Legislature all the supremacy to which it is entitled, we cannot yield to it the omnipotence which has been ascribed to the British Parliament, so long as we have a Constitution which limits its powers, and places certain innate rights of the citizen beyond its control.

It is said that the first section of Article first of the Constitution is a commonplace assertion of a general principle, and was not intended as a restriction upon the power of the Legislature. This court has not so considered it.

In Billings *vs.* Hall (7 Cal. 1), Chief Justice Murray says, in reference to this section of the Constitution: "This principle is as old as the Magna Charta. It lies at the foundation of every constitutional government, and is necessary to the existence of civil liberty and free institutions. It was not lightly incorporated into the Constitution of this State, as one of those political dogmas designed to tickle the popular ear, and conveying no substantial meaning or idea, but as one of those fundamental principles of enlightened government, without a rigorous observance of which there could be neither liberty nor safety to the citizen."

In the same case, Mr. Justice Burnett asserted the following principles, which bear directly upon the question:—

"That among the inalienable rights declared by our Constitution as belonging to each citizen, is a right of 'acquiring, possessing, and protecting property.' ... 'That for the Constitution to declare a right inalienable, and at the same time leave the Legislature unlimited power over it, would be [103] a contradiction in terms, an idle provision, proving that a Constitution was a mere parchment barrier, insufficient to protect the citizen, delusive, and visionary, and the practical result of which would be to destroy, not conserve, the rights it vainly assumed to protect.'"

Upon this point I dissent from the opinion of the court in Billings *vs.* Hall, and if I considered the question an open one, I might yet doubt its correctness, but the doctrine announced in that opinion having received the sanction of the majority of the court, has become the rule of decision, and it is the duty of the court to see it is uniformly enforced, and that its application is not confined to a particular class of cases.

It is the settled doctrine of this court to enforce every provision of the Constitution in favor of the rights reserved to the citizens against a usurpation of power in any question whatsoever; and although in a doubtful case we would yield to the authority of the Legislature, yet upon the question before us we are constrained to declare that, in our opinion, the Act in question is in conflict with the first section of Article first of the Constitution, because, without necessity, it infringes upon the liberty of the citizen, by restraining his right to acquire property.

And that it is in conflict with the fourth section of the same article because it was intended as, and is in effect, a discrimination in favor of one religious profession, and gives it a preference over all others.

It follows that the petitioner was improperly convicted, and it is ordered that he be discharged from custody.

Burnett, J.—The great importance of the constitutional principle involved, and the different view I take of some points, make it proper for me to submit a separate opinion. The question is one of no ordinary magnitude, and of great intrinsic difficulty. The embarrassment we might otherwise experience in deciding a question of such interest to the community, and in reference to which there exists so great a difference of opinion, is increased by the consideration that the weight of the adjudged cases is against the conclusion at which we have been compelled to arrive.

In considering this constitutional question it must be conceded that there are some great leading principles of justice, eternal and unchangeable, that are applicable at all times and under all circumstances. It is upon this basis that all Constitutions of free government must rest. A Constitution that admits that there are any inalienable rights of human nature reserved to the individual, and not ceded to society, must, of logical necessity, concede the truth of this position. But it is equally true that there are other principles, the application of which may be justly modified by circumstances.

It would seem to be true that exact justice is only an exact conformity to some law. Without law there could be neither merit nor demerit, justice nor injustice; and when we come to decide the question whether a given act be just or unjust, we must keep in our view that system of law by [104] which we judge it. As judged by one code of law, the act may be innocent; while as judged by another, it may be criminal. As judged by the system of abstract justice (which is only that code of law which springs from the natural relation and fitness of things), there must be certain inherent and inalienable rights of human nature that no government can rightfully take away. These rights are retained by the individual because their surrender is not required by the good of the whole. The just and legitimate ends of civil government can be practically and efficiently accomplished whilst these rights are retained by the individual. Every person, upon entering into a state of society, only surrenders so much of his individual rights as may be necessary to secure the substantial happiness of the community. Whatever is not necessary to attain this end is reserved to himself.

But, conceding the entire correctness of these views, it must be equally clear that the original and primary jurisdiction to determine the question what are these inalienable rights, must exist somewhere; and wherever placed, its exercise must be conclusive, in the contemplation of the theory, upon all.

The power to decide what individual right must be conceded to society, originally existed in the sovereign people who made the Constitution. As they possessed this primary and original jurisdiction, their action must be final. If they exercised this power, in whole or in part, in the formation of the Constitution, their action, so far, is conclusive.

It must also be conceded that this power, from its very nature, must be legislative and not judicial. The question is simply one of necessity—of abstract justice. It is a question that naturally enters into the mind of the law-maker, not into that of the law-expounder. The judicial power, from the nature of its functions, cannot determine such a question. Judicial justice is but conformity to the law as already made.

If these views be correct, the judicial department cannot, in any case, go behind the Constitution, and by any original standard judge the justice or legality of any single one or more of its provisions. The judiciary is but the creature of the Constitution, and cannot judge its creator. It cannot rise above the source of its own existence. If it could do this, it could annul the Constitution, instead of simply declaring what it means. And the same may be said of any act of the Legislature, if within the limits of its discretion as defined by the Constitution. Such an act of the Legislature is as much beyond the reach of the judiciary as is the Constitution itself. (1 Bald. 74; 1 Brock. 203; 10 Pet. 478; 5 Geo. 194.)

But it is the right and imperative duty of this court to construe the Constitution and statutes in the last resort, and from that construction, to ascertain the will of the law-maker. And the only legitimate purpose for which a court can resort to the principles of abstract justice, is to ascertain the proper construction of the law in cases of doubt. When, in the opinion of the court, a given construction is clearly contrary to the manifest principles [105] of justice, then it will be presumed, is a case not free from doubt that the Legislature never intended such a consequence. (Varick *vs*. Briggs, 6 Paige, 330; Flint River Steamboat Company *vs*. Foster. 5 Geo. 194.) But when the intention is clear, however unjust and absurd the consequences may be, it must prevail, unless it contravenes a constitutional provision.

If these views be correct, it follows that there can be for this court no higher law than the Constitution; and in determining this question of constitutional construction, we must forget, as far as in us lies, that we are religious or irreligious men. It is solely a matter of construction, with which our individual feelings, prejudices, or opinions upon abstract questions of justice can have nothing to do. The Constitution may have been unwisely framed. It may have given too much or too little power to the Legislature. But these are questions for the statesman, not for the jurist. Courts are bound by the law as it is.

The British Constitution differs from our American Constitution in one great leading feature. It only classifies and distributes, but does not limit the powers of government; while our Constitutions do both. It is believed that this difference has been sometimes overlooked by our courts in considering constitutional questions; and English authorities followed in cases to which they could not be properly applied. We often meet with the expression that Christianity is a part of the common law. Conceding that this is true, it is not perceived how it can influence the decision of a constitutional question. The Constitution of this State will not tolerate any discrimination or preference in favor of any religion; and so far as the common law conflicts with this provision, it must yield to the Constitution. Our constitutional theory regards all religions, as such, equally entitled to protection, and all equally unentitled to any preference. Before the Constitution they are all equal. In so far as the principles found in all, or in any one or more of the different religious systems, are considered applicable to the ends legitimately contemplated by civil constitutional government, they can be embodied in our laws and enforced. But when there is no ground or necessity upon which a principle can rest, but a religious one, then the Constitution steps in, and says that you shall not enforce it by authority of law.

The Constitution says that "the free exercise and enjoyment of religious profession and worship, without discrimination or preference, shall forever be allowed in this State."

If we give this language a mere literal construction, we must conclude that the protection given is only intended for the professor, and not for him who does not worship. "The free exercise and enjoyment of religious profession and worship," is the thing expressly protected by the Constitution. But taking the whole section together, it is clear that the scope and purpose of the Constitution was to assert the great, broad principle of religious freedom for all—for the believer and the unbeliever. The Government [106] has no more power to punish a citizen when he professes no religion, than it has to punish him when he professes any particular religion.

The Act of the Legislature under consideration violates this section of the Constitution, because it establishes a compulsory religious observance; and not, as I conceive, because it makes a discrimination between different systems of religion. If it be true that the Constitution intended to secure entire religious freedom to all, without regard to the fact whether they were believers or unbelievers, then it follows that the Legislature could not create and enforce any merely religious observance whatever. It was the purpose of the Constitution to establish a *permanent* principle, applicable at all times, under all circumstances, and to all persons. If all the people of the State had been unbelievers, the Act would have been subject to the same objection. So, if they had been all Christians, the power of the Legislature to pass the Act would equally have been wanting. The will of the whole people has been expressed through the Constitution; and until his expression of their will has been changed in some authoritative form, it must prevail with all the departments of the State Government. The Constitution, from its very nature as a permanent, organic Act, could not shape its provisions so as to meet the changing views of individuals. Had the Act made Monday, instead of Sunday, a day of compulsory rest, the constitutional question would have been the same. The fact that the Christian *voluntarily* keeps holy the first day of the week, does not authorize the Legislature to make that observance *compulsory*. The Legislature cannot compel the citizen to do that which the Constitution leaves him free to do or omit, at his election. The Act violates as much the religious freedom of the Christian as of the Jew. Because the conscientious views of the Christian compel him to keep Sunday as a Sabbath, he has the right to object, when the Legislature invades his freedom of religious worship, and assumes the power to compel him to do that which he has the right to omit if he pleases. The principle is the same, whether the Act of the Legislature *compels* us to do that which we wish to do or not to do.

The *compulsory* power does not exist in either case. If the Legislature has power over the subject, this power exists without regard to the particular views of the individuals. The sole inquiry with us is whether the Legislature can create a day of compulsory rest. If the Legislature has the power, then it has the right to select the particular day. It could not well do otherwise.

The protection of the Constitution extends to *every* individual, or to none. It is the individual that is intended to be protected. The principle is the same, whether the many or the few are concerned. The Constitution did not mean to inquire how many or how few would profess or not profess this or that particular religion. If there be but a single individual in the State who professes a particular faith, he is as much within the sacred protection of the Constitution as if he agreed with the great majority [107] of his fellow-citizens. We cannot, therefore, inquire into the particular views of the petitioner, or of any other individual. We are not bound to take judicial notice of such matters, and they are not matters of proof. There may be individuals in the State that hold Monday as a Sabbath. If there be none such now, there may be in the future. And if the unconstitutionality of an Act of this character depended, in any manner, upon the fact that a particular day of the week was selected, then it follows that any individual could defeat the Act by professing to hold the day specified as his Sabbath. The Constitution protects the freedom of religious *profession* and *worship*, without regard to the sincerity or insincerity of the worshiper. We could not inquire into the fact whether the individual professing to hold a particular day as his Sabbath was sincere or otherwise. He has the right to profess and worship as he pleases, without having his motives inquired into. His motives in exercising a constitutional privilege are matters too sacred to be submitted to judicial scrutiny. Every citizen has the undoubted right to vote and worship as he pleases, without having his motives impeached in any tribunal of the State.

Under the Constitution of this State, the Legislature cannot pass any Act, the legitimate effect of which is *forcibly* to establish any merely religious truth, or enforce any merely religious observances. The Legislature has no power over such a subject. When, therefore, the citizen is sought to be compelled by the Legislature to do any affirmative religious act, or to refrain from doing anything, because it violates simply a religious principle or observance, the Act is unconstitutional.

In considering the question whether the Act can be sustained upon the ground that it is a mere municipal regulation, the inquiry as to the reasons which operated upon the minds of members in voting for the measure is, as I conceive, wholly immaterial. The constitutional question is a naked question of legislative power. Had the Legislature the power to do the particular thing done? What was that particular thing? It was the prohibition of labor on Sunday. Had the Act been so framed as to show that it was intended by those who voted for it, as simply a municipal regulation; yet, if, in fact, it contravened the provision of the Constitution securing religious freedom to all, we should have been compelled to declare it unconstitutional for *that* reason. So, the fact that the Act is so framed as to show that a different reason operated upon the minds of those who voted for it, will not prevent us from sustaining the Act, if any portion of the Constitution conferred the power to pass it upon the Legislature.

Where the power exists to do a particular thing, and the thing is done, the reason which induced the act is not to be inquired into by the courts. The power may be abused; but the abuse of the power cannot be avoided by the judiciary. A court may give a wrong reason for a proper judgment; still the judgment must stand. The members of the Legislature may vote for a particular measure from erroneous or improper motives. [108] The only question with the courts is, whether that body had the power to command the particular Act to be done or omitted. The view here advanced, is sustained substantially by the decision in the case of Fletcher *vs.* Peck (6 Cranch, 131).

It was urged, in argument, that the provision of the first section of the first Article of the Constitution, asserting the "inalienable right of acquiring, possessing, and protecting property," was only the statement in general terms, on a general principle, not capable in its nature of being judicially enforced.

It will be observed that the first Article contains a declaration of rights, and if the first section of that Article asserts a principle not susceptible of practical application, then it may admit of a question whether any principle asserted in this declaration of rights can be the subject of judicial enforcement. But that at least a portion of the general principles asserted in that Article can be enforced by judicial determination, must be conceded. This has been held at all times, by all the courts, so far as I am informed.

The provisions of the sixteenth section of the first Article, which prohibits the Legislature from passing any law impairing the obligation of contracts, is based essentially upon the same ground as the first section, which asserts the right to acquire, possess, and defend property. The right substantially secured by both sections is the right of property. This right of property is the substantial basis upon which the provisions of both sections must rest. The reason of, and the end to be accomplished by, each section, are the same. The debtor has received property or other valuable consideration for the sum he owes the creditor, and the sum, when collected by the creditor, becomes his property. The right of the creditor to collect from the debtor that which is due, is essentially a right of property. It is the right to obtain from the debtor property which is unjustly detained from the creditor.

If we take the position to be true, for the sake of the argument, that the right of property cannot be enforced by the courts against an Act of the Legislature, we then concede a power that renders the restrictions of other sections inoperative. For example, if the Legislature has the power to take the property of one citizen and give it to another without compensation, the prohibition to pass any law impairing the obligation of contracts could readily be avoided. All the Legislature would have to do to accomplish this purpose, would be to allow the creditor first to collect his debt, and afterward take the property of the creditor and give it to the debtor. For if we once concede the power of the Legislature to take the property of A and give it to B, without compensation, we must concede to that body the exclusive right to judge when, and in what instances, this conceded right should be exercised.

It was also insisted, in argument, that the judicial enforcement of the right of property, as asserted in the first section, is inconsistent with [109] the power of compulsory process, to enforce the collection of debts by the seizure and sale of the property of the debtor. But is this true? On the contrary, is not the power to seize and sell the property of the debtor expressly given by the Constitution for the very purpose of protecting and enforcing this right of property? When the Constitution says that you shall not impair the obligation of the contract, it says in direct effect that you shall enforce it; and the only means to do this efficiently is by a seizure and sale. The seizure and sale of the property of the debtor was contemplated by the Constitution, as being a part of the contract itself. The debtor stipulates in the contract, that, in case he fails to pay, the creditor may seize and sell his property by legal process. Such is the legal effect of the contract, because the existing law enters into and forms a part of it.

The different provisions of the Constitution will be found, when fairly and justly considered, to be harmonious and mutually dependent one upon the other. A general principle may be asserted in one section without any specification of the exceptions in that place. But it must be evident that practical convenience and logical arrangement will not always permit the exceptions to be stated in the same section. It is a matter of no importance in what part of the Constitution the exception may be found. Wherever found, it must be taken from the general rule, leaving the remainder of the rule to stand. The general right of enjoying and defending life and liberty is asserted in the first section of the first Article; while the exceptions are stated in the eighth, ninth, fifteenth, and eighteenth sections of the same Article. A party may, by express provisions of the Constitution, forfeit his liberty. The same remark in reference to exceptions to general principles, will apply to other provisions.

The right to protect and possess property is not more clearly protected by the Constitution than the right to acquire. The right to acquire must include the right to use the proper means to attain the end. The right itself would be impotent without the power to use its necessary incidents. The Legislature, therefore, cannot prohibit the proper use of the means of acquiring property, except the peace and safety of the State require it. And in reference to this point, I adopt the reasons given by the Chief Justice, and concur in the views expressed by him.

There are certain classes of subjects over which the Legislature possesses a wide discretion; but still this discretion is confined within certain limits; and although, from the complex nature of the subject, these limits cannot always be definitely settled in advance, they do and must exist. It was long held, in general terms, that the Legislature had the power to regulate the remedy; but cases soon arose where the courts were compelled to interpose. In the case of Bronson *vs.* Kenzie (1 How. 311), Chief Justice Taney uses this clear language:—

"It is difficult, perhaps, to draw a line that would be applicable in all cases, between legitimate alterations of the remedy and provisions which in [110] the form of remedy impair the right; but it is manifest that the obligation of the contract may, in effect, be destroyed by denying a remedy altogether; or may be seriously impaired by hampering the proceedings with new conditions and restrictions, so as to make the remedy hardly worth pursuing."

So, the power of the Legislature to pass Recording Acts and Statutes of Limitations is conceded, in general terms, and a wide discretion given. Yet, in reference to these powers, Mr. Justice Baldwin, in delivering the opinion of the Supreme Court of the United States, in the case of Jackson *vs.* Lamphine (3 Pet. 289), uses this language:—

"Cases may occur where the provisions of a law on these subjects may be so unreasonable as to amount to a denial of the right and call for the interposition of the court."

The Legislature is vested by the Constitution with a wide discretion in determining what is necessary to the peace and safety of the State; yet this discretion has some limits. It may be difficult, in many cases, to define these limits with exact precision; but this difficulty cannot show that there are no limits. Such difficulties must arise under every system of limited government.

The question arising under this Act is quite distinguishable from the case where the Legislature of a State in which slavery is tolerated, passes an Act for the protection of the slave against the inhumanity of the master in not allowing sufficient rest. In this State, every man is a free agent, competent and able to protect himself, and no one is bound by law to labor for any particular person. Free agents must be left free, as to themselves. Had the Act under consideration been confined to infants or persons bound by law to obey others, then the question presented would have been very different. But if we cannot trust agents to regulate their own labor, its times and quantity, it is difficult to trust them to make their own contracts. If the Legislature could prescribe the days of rest for them, then it would seem that the same power could prescribe the hours to work, rest, and eat.

For these reasons, I concur with the Chief Justice in discharging the petitioner. [111]

Decision and Dictum of Judge Hammond, In Re King

We reprint herewith also Judge Hammond's decision and *dictum* in full. It is only fair that we should do this, that the reader may examine together and for himself both the decision and our review of it. It is well, also, to print it, that as many as possible of the people may see for themselves how far from the principles that are intended to guide and govern the Courts of the United States, a judge of one of these Courts is ready to go to conform to what he supposes to be public opinion, and to sustain a religious party in a "factitious advantage" which has been acquired and which is maintained "in spite of the clamor for religious freedom and the progress that has been made in the absolute separation of Church and State."

Hammond, J.: The petitioner, R. M. King, was in due form indicted in the Circuit Court of Obion county for that "he then and there unlawfully and unnecessarily engaged in his secular business and performed his common avocation of life, to wit, plowing on Sunday," which said working was charged to be "a common nuisance." Upon a formal trial by a jury he was convicted and fined $75, which conviction was, upon appeal, affirmed by the Supreme Court, and the fine not being paid, he was imprisoned, all in due form of law.

He thereupon sued this writ of *habeas corpus*, alleging that he is held in custody in violation of the Constitution of the United States, and the sheriff of Obion county sets up in defense of the writ the legal proceedings aforesaid under which he has custody of the prisoner. The petitioner moves for his discharge upon the ground that he is held in violation of the Fourteenth Amendment of the Constitution. He proves that he is a Seventh-day Adventist, keeps Saturday according to his creed, and works on Sunday for that reason alone.

The contention is "that there is not any law in Tennessee" to justify the conviction which was had, and that the proceedings must be not only in legal form, but likewise grounded upon a law of the State, statute or common, making the conduct complained of by the indictment, an offense; otherwise the imprisonment is arbitrary, and "without due process of law," just as effectually within the purview of the Fourteenth Amendment as if the method of procedure had been illegal and void. If there be no law in Tennessee, statute or common, making the act of working on Sunday a nuisance, then, indeed, the conviction is void; for the Amendment is not merely a restraint upon arbitrary procedure in its form, but also in its substance; and however strictly legal and orderly the court may have proceeded to conviction, if the act done was not a crime, as charged, there has been no "due process of law" to deprive the person of his liberty. This is undoubtedly the result of the adjudicated cases, and it is not necessary to cite them. [112]

It is also true that Congress has furnished the aggrieved person with a remedy by writ of *habeas corpus* to enforce in the Federal Courts the restrictions of this amendment, and to protect him against arbitrary imprisonment, in the sense just mentioned; but it has not and could not constitute those courts tribunals of review, to reverse and set aside the convictions in the State Courts, that may be illegal in the sense that they are founded on an erroneous judgment as to what the statute or common law of the State may be. If so, every conviction in the State Courts would be reversible in the Federal Courts where errors of law could be assigned. To say that there is an absence of any law to justify the prosecution, is only to say that the court has erred in declaring the law to be that the thing done is criminal under the law, and all errors of law import an absence of law to justify the judgment. I do not think the amendment or the *habeas corpus* act has conferred upon this court the power to overhaul the decisions of the State Courts of Tennessee, and determine whether they have, in a given case, rightly adjudged the law of the State to have affixed a criminal quality to the given act of the petitioner.

It is urged that if the judgment of conviction by the State Court be held conclusive of the law in the given case, the Amendment and the Act of Congress are emasculated, and there can be no inquiry, in any case, of value to him who is imprisoned, as to whether he is deprived of his liberty without due process of law; that the Federal Court must necessarily make an independent inquiry to see whether there be any law, statute or common, upon which to found the conviction; or else the prisoner is remediless under federal law to redress a violation of this guaranty of the Federal Constitution. It is said that we make the same inquiry into the law of the State under the Fourteenth Amendment that we do into the law of the United States under the Fifth Amendment, containing precisely the same guaranty against the arbitrary exercise of federal power, and that the one is as plenary as the other; that this case does not fall within the category of those wherein by act of Congress the Federal Courts must give effect to local law as declared by the State tribunals; and that, while we may not review errors of judgment, we must, in execution of this amendment, vacate, by relief on *habeas corpus*, any void judgment or sentence—made void by the amendment itself.

The court concedes fully the soundness of this position, but not the application of it. It is quite difficult to draw the line of demarkation here between a line of judgment that shall protect the integrity of the State Courts against impertinent review, and maintain the full measure of federal power in giving effect to the amendments; but, as has been said in other cases of like perplexity, we must confine our efforts to define the power and its limitations within the boundaries required for the careful adjudication of actual cases as they arise; and I think it more important still that we shall not overlook the fact that we have a dual and complex system of government, which fact of itself and by its necessary implications, must modify the argument of such questions as this, by conforming it to that fact itself. And we find here in this case an easy path out of this perplexity by doing this.

Let us imagine a State without any common law, and only a statutory code of criminal law,—and we have an example at hand in our Federal State,—where we are accustomed to say the United States has no common law of crimes, and he who accuses one of any offense must put his finger on some act of Congress denouncing that particular conduct as criminal. If [113] we were making the very inquiry so much argued in this case, whether it can be punishable as a crime to work in one's field on Sunday, within the domain of federal jurisprudence, say under the Fifth Amendment instead of the Fourteenth Amendment, it would be easily resolved, and the prisoner would be discharged; unless the respondent could point to a statute making it so, and precisely according to the accusation or indictment. If such a simple condition of law existed in the State of Tennessee, we could have no trouble with this case. But it does not. There we have a vast body of unwritten laws, civil and criminal, as to which an entirely different method of ascertaining what is and what is not law obtains. What is that method? It is not essential to go into any legal casuistry to determine whether, when a point of common law first arises for adjudication, the judges who declare it make the law, or only testify to the usage or custom which we call law; for it is equally binding in either case as a declaration, [1 Blk., 69.] The judges are the depositaries of that law, just as the statute book is the depository of the statute law; and when they speak, the law is established, and none can gainsay it. They have the power, for grave reasons, to change an adjudication and re-establish the point, even reversely, but generally are bound and do adhere to the first precedent. This is "due process of law" in that matter. Moreover, when the mooted point has been finally adjudicated between the parties, it is absolutely conclusive as between them. Other parties in other cases may have the decision reversed, as a precedent for all subsequent cases; but there is no remedy in that case or for that party, unless it may be by executive clemency, if a criminal case, against the erroneous declaration of the law. In that celebrated "disquisition," as he calls it in the preface, of Mr. Jefferson, in which he so angrily combats the *dictum* of Sir Matthew Hale, that "Christianity is parcel of the laws of England," he accurately expresses this principle in these words: "But in later times we take no judge's word for what the law is, further than is warranted by the authorities he appeals to. His decision may bind the unfortunate individual who happens to be the particular subject of it; but it cannot alter the law. [Jeff. Rep. (Va.) Appdx., 139.] And Mr. Chief Justice Clayton, in his equally celebrated reply to Mr. Jefferson, states that this was the very point decided by the case cited from the Year Books [34 H. 6, 38], by Mr. Jefferson and misunderstood by him; namely, that when the ecclesiastical court in a case within its jurisdiction had decided a given matter, the common law of England recognized it as conclusive when collaterally called in question in the common law courts. [State *vs.* Chandler, 2 Harr., 553, 559.]

But the application of this principle should not be misunderstood here, and it should be remembered that in a case like this we apply it as a matter of evidence. The verdict of the jury and the judgment of the State Circuit Court thereon, and its affirmance by the Supreme Court of Tennessee (a mere incident this affirmance is, however, in the sense we are now considering the principle), is to us here, and to all elsewhere, necessarily conclusive testimony as to what the common law of Tennessee is in the matter of King's plowing in his fields on the Sundays mentioned in the indictment and proved in the record. As to the petitioner, whether he be an unfortunate victim of an erroneous verdict and decision or not, it is due process of law, and according to the law of the land, that he shall be bound by it everywhere except in a court competent to review and reverse the verdict and the judgment upon it; and surely it was not the intention of the [114] Fourteenth Amendment to confer upon this court or any other Federal Court of any degree whatever, that power. It was due process of law for the jury having him properly in hand, to render the verdict and for the court to pass judgment upon it; and the declaration of the judges that to do that which he did was a common nuisance according to the common law of Tennessee, is conclusive evidence, as to that act of his, that it was so. This is not holding that the Federal Courts shall not, upon a *habeas corpus*, inquire independently as to whether the act complained of was a crime as charged in the indictment or not, but only that in making that inquiry, however independently, the verdict and judgment, if the State Court had jurisdiction and the procedure has been regular, must be conclusive evidence on the point of law. It is not binding, like the decisions which are rules of property are binding, because our federal statute says they shall be; nor like a matter of local law, which the Federal Courts administer, because it is local law and binding between the parties—these are inherently binding on us; but binding as we are bound by the unimpeachable testimony of a witness, as we are bound by the conclusive evidence of the certificate of the Secretary of State that certain given words constitute a statute of the State, or by the printed and authorized book of statutes, or by our judicial notice which we take that certain given words do constitute a statute, or as we might under some circumstances be bound by the oral testimony of witnesses as to what is the law of a foreign state. In the very nature of the common law, and, indeed, as that very "due process of law" after which we are looking so concernedly in this case, this principle is fundamental. We have no other possible method of ascertaining what is the common law of Tennessee in this case than that of looking to the verdict and judgment as our witness of it. If we go to former precedents and other authorities, like those of the opinions of the sages and text-writers, we do that which no other court has power to do, in that case, except the court which had pending before it the indictment and the plea of the defendant thereto, making the technical issue as to what the law of the case was; and we usurp the functions of the trial judge, and jury, or of the appellate court having authority to review the trial judge, and jury.

It is my opinion that this principle reaches even further than this, and that, evidentially, we are quite as conclusively bound, upon this independent inquiry we are making, by the testimony of the decision of Parker *vs.* the State [16 Lee, 476], that it is a common nuisance in Tennessee, according to its common law, to work on Sunday; notwithstanding it somewhat ignominiously overrules, without mentioning it, the former precedents in that court, of the State *vs.* Long [7 Baxter, 95]; because it is likewise a part of the principle itself that the last precedent is controlling; and we do not, as suggested by counsel, take this conflict of precedent as authorizing an independent judgment, as we do in an entirely different class of cases involving the construction of contracts made by the State in the form of statutes. In that class of cases it is a mere conflict of opinion as to the intention of the parties in using certain words in their form of contract, generally as much open to the Federal as the State Courts, where the conflict has resulted in diverse opinions; but here there is not any such latitude of action, because of the conclusive effect of a precedent at common law as evidence of the common law itself. This is what the Supreme Court means when it says, in cases like this and other cases there by writ of error from the State courts, that we are bound by the decisions of the State [115] Courts as to the criminal laws of the State. Whether it be a question as to whether there be a common-law crime or an offense under the proper construction of a doubtful statute, or whether the Constitution of the State has been properly construed, it is all the same. Re Duncan, 139 U. S., 449; Leeper *vs.* Texas, Ib. 462, 467; Baldwin vs. Kansas, 129 United States, 52; and numerous other cases of like import might be cited. The result of them all is that in enforcing the Fourteenth Amendment the Federal Courts will confine themselves to the function of seeing that the fundamental principle—that the citizen shall not be arbitrarily proceeded against contrary to the usual course of the law in such cases, nor punished without authority of law, nor unequally, and the like—shall not be violated in any given case; but they will not substitute their judgment for that of the State Courts as to what are the laws of the State in any case. A proper adjustment of the two parts of our dual system of government requires this, and the utmost care should be taken not to impair the rightful operations of the State Government, although they may, in a given case, appear to have wrought injustice or oppression. No government is free from such misfortunes occasionally arising, nor should they ever provoke the greater misfortune of the usurpation of unauthorized power by either of the branches of our system—State or Federal. This view of the case disposes of it; for when the petitioner was, by lawful process, arraigned upon indictment, and by lawful trial convicted of a crime in a court having the lawful right to declare his conduct to have been a crime, he has had "due process of law," and has been made to suffer "according to the law of the land," albeit the court may have made a mistake of fact or law in the progress of that particular administration of the "law of the land." That mistake we cannot correct, nor can any court after final judgment; and this itself is one of the fundamental principles essential to be preserved as one of the elements of that "due process of law" secured by the Fourteenth Amendment.

Perhaps this judgment should end here, and that, technically, nothing more should be said. Yet it may be due to counsel to give some response to their extended and really very able arguments upon other questions which they think are involved, and which they wish to have decided in this case. As we do not refuse their motion to discharge the petitioner because of any want of jurisdiction, but only because we decide that he has not been convicted without due process of law, as he alleges, it may not be improper, and, at least, it will emphasize our judicial allegiance to the principle already adverted to of the conclusiveness, as a matter of evidence, of the verdict against him, if we say that but for that allegiance we should have no difficulty in thinking that King has been wrongfully convicted. Not because he has any guaranty under the Federal or State Constitutions against a law denouncing him and punishing him for a nuisance in working on Sunday; for he has not. It was a belief of Mr. Madison and other founders of our Government that they had practically established absolute religious freedom and exemption from persecution for opinion's sake in matters of religion; but while they made immense strides in that direction, and the subsequent progress in freedom of thought has advanced the liberalism of the conception these founders had, as a matter of fact, they left to the States the most absolute power on the subject, and any of them might, if they chose, establish a creed and a church, and maintain it. The most they did, as they confessed, was to set a good example by the Federal Constitution; and happily that example has been substantially followed in this matter, and by no State [116] more thoroughly than Tennessee, where sectarian freedom of religious belief is guaranteed by the Constitution; not in the sense argued here, that King as a Seventh-day Adventist, or some other as a Jew, or yet another as a Seventh-day Baptist, might set at defiance the prejudices, if you please, of other sects having control of legislation in the matter of Sunday observances, but only in the sense that he should not himself be disturbed in the practices of his creed; which is quite a different thing from saying that in the course of his daily labor, disconnected with his religion, just as much as other people's labor is disconnected with their religion, labor not being an acknowledged principle or tenet of religion by him, nor generally or anywhere, he might disregard laws made in aid, if you choose to say so, of the religion of other sects. We say, not acknowledged by him, because, although he testifies that the fourth commandment is as binding in its direction for labor on six days of the week as for rest on the seventh, he does not prove that that notion is held as a part of the creed of his sect and religiously observed as such, and we know, historically, that generally it has not been so considered by any religionists or their teachers. But if a nonconformist of any kind should enter the church of another sect, and those assembled there were required, every one of them, to comply with a certain ceremony, he could not discourteously refuse because his mode was different, or because he did not believe in the divine sanction of that ceremony, and rely upon this constitutional guaranty to protect his refusal. We do not say Sunday observance may be compelled upon this principle, as a religious act, but only illustrate that the constitutional guaranty of religious freedom does not afford the measure of duty under such circumstances, nor does it any more, it seems to us, protect the citizen in refusing to conform to Sunday ordinances. It was not intended to have that effect any more than under our Federal Constitution the polygamist may defy the Christian laws against bigamy upon the ground of religious feeling or sentiment, the freedom of which has been guaranteed.

Nor do we believe King was wrongfully convicted because Christianity is not a part of the law of the land; for in the sense pointed out by Mr. Chief-Justice Clayton in State *vs.* Chandler, *supra*, and more recently by Dr. Anderson, a clergyman, before the Social Science Association [20 Alb. L. J., 265, 285], it surely is; but not in the dangerous sense so forcibly combated by Mr. Jefferson and other writers following him in the controversy over it. The fourth commandment is neither a part of the common law or the statute, and disobedience to it is not punishable by law; and certainly the substitution of the first day of the week for the seventh as a part of the commandment has not been accomplished by municipal process, and the substitution is not binding as such. The danger that lurks in this application of the aphorism has been noted by every intelligent writer under my observation, and all agree that this commandment, either in its original form, as practiced by petitioner, or in its substituted application to the first day of the week, is not more a part of our common law than the doctrine of the Trinity or the apostles' creed. Nevertheless, by a sort of factitious advantage, the observers of Sunday have secured the aid of the civil law, and adhere to that advantage with great tenacity, in spite of the clamor for religious freedom, and the progress that has been made in the absolute separation of Church and State; and in spite of the strong and merciless attack that has always been ready, in the field of controversial theology, to be made, as it has been made here, upon the claim for divine [117] authority for the change from the seventh to the first day of the week. Volumes have been written upon that subject, and it is not useful to attempt to add anything to it here. We have no tribunals for its decision, and the efforts to extirpate the advantage above mentioned by judicial decision in favor of a civil right to disregard the change, seem to me quite useless. The proper appeal is to the Legislature. For the courts cannot change that which has been done, however done, by the civil law in favor of the Sunday observers. The religion of Jesus Christ is so interwoven with the texture of our civilization and every one of its institutions, that it is impossible for any man or set of men to live among us and find exemption from its influences and restraints. Sunday observance is so essentially a part of that religion that it is impossible to rid our laws of it, quite as impossible as to abolish the custom we have of using the English language, or clothing ourselves with the garments appropriate to our sex. The logic of personal liberty would allow, perhaps demand, a choice of garments, but the choice is denied. So civil or religious freedom may stop short of its logic in this matter of Sunday observance. It is idle to expect in government perfect action or harmony of essential principles, and whoever administers, whoever makes, and whoever executes the laws, must take into account the imperfections, the passions, the prejudices, religious or other, and the errings of men because of these. We cannot have in individual cases a perfect observance of Sunday, according to the rules of religion; and, indeed, the sects are at war with each other as to the modes of observance. And yet no wise man will say that there shall be, therefore, no observance at all. Government leaves the warring sects to observe as they will, so they do not disturb each other; and as to the non-observer, he cannot be allowed his fullest personal freedom in all respects; largely he is allowed to do as he pleases, and generally there is no pursuit of him, in these days, as a mere matter of disciplining his conscience; but only when he defiantly sets up his non-observance by ostentatious display of his disrespect for the feelings or prejudices of others.

If the human impulse to rest on as many days as one can have for rest from toil, is not adequate, as it usually is, to secure abstention from daily vocations on Sunday, one may, and many thousands do, work on that day, without complaint from any source; but if one ostentatiously labors for the purpose of emphasizing his distaste for or his disbelief in the custom, he may be made to suffer for his defiance by persecutions, if you call them so, on the part of the great majority, who will compel him to rest when they rest, as it does in many other instances compel men to yield individual tastes to the public taste, sometimes by positive law, and sometimes by a universal public opinion and practice far more potential than a formal statute. There is scarcely any man who has not had to yield something to this law of the majority, which is itself a universal law from which we cannot escape in the name of equal rights or civil liberty. As before remarked, one may not discard his garments and appear without them, or in those not belonging to the sex, and this illustration is used rather than others frequently given based on the laws of sanitation, education, immoral practices, cruelty, blasphemy, and the like, because it seems somewhat freer from the inherent element of injury to others, and contains likewise the element of a selection that would seem to be harmless in itself; so that it illustrates, pertinently, that one must observe the general custom as to a day of public rest, just as he must reasonably wear the garments of [118] his sex selected by general custom. Therefore, while out of our 64,000,000 people there are a comparatively very few thousands who prefer the seven h day to the first as a day of rest and for religious observances, according to the strict letter of the commandment, and who, possibly with good reason, resent the change that has been made as being without divine sanction, the fact remains that the change has been made by almost universal custom, and they must conform to it so far as it relates to its quality as a day of public rest.

And here it may be noted that sometimes too little heed is given in the consideration of the question to this quality of associated rest from labor. It is not altogether an individual matter of benefit from the rest, for undoubtedly to each individual one day of the seven would answer as well as another; but it is the benefit to the population of a general and aggregate cessation from labor on a given day, which the law would secure, because for good reason, no doubt, found in our practice of it, it is beneficial to the population to do this thing, and they have established the custom to do it. The fact that religious belief is one of the foundations of the custom is no objection to it, as long as the individual is not compelled to observe the religious ceremonies others choose to observe in connection with their rest days.

As we said in the outset, not one of our laws or institutions or customs is free from the influence of our religion, and that religion has put our race and people in the very front of all nations in everything that makes the human race comfortable and useful in the world. This very principle of religious freedom is the product of our religion, as all of our good customs are; and if it be desirable to extend that principle to the ultimate condition that no man shall be in the least restrained, by law or public opinion, in hostility to religion itself, or in the exhibition of individual eccentricities or practices of sectarian peculiarities of religious observances of any kind, or be fretted with laws colored by any religion that is distasteful to anybody, those who desire that condition must necessarily await its growth into that enlarged application. But the courts cannot, in cases like this, ignore the existing customs and laws of the masses, nor their prejudices and passions even, to lift the individual out of the restraints surrounding him because of those customs and laws, before the time has come when public opinion shall free all men in the manner desired. Therefore it is that the petitioner cannot shelter himself just yet behind the doctrine of religious freedom in defying the existence of a law and its application to him, which is distasteful to his own religious feeling or fanaticism, that the seventh day of the week, instead of the first, should be set apart by the public for the day of public rest and religious practices. That is what he really believes and wishes, he and his sect, and not that each individual shall select his own day of public rest and his own day of labor. His real complaint is, that his adversaries on this point have the advantage of usage and custom, and the laws founded on that usage and custom, not that religious freedom has been denied to him. He does not belong to the class that would abrogate all laws for a day of rest, because the day of rest is useful to religion, and aids in maintaining its churches; for none more than he professes the sanctifying influence of the fourth commandment, the literal observance of which, by himself and all men, is the distinguishing demand of his own peculiar sect. His demand for religious freedom is as disingenuous here as is the argument of his adversary sects that it is the economic value of the day of rest, [119] and not its religious character which they would preserve by civil law. The truth is, both are dominated by their religious controversy over the day, but like all other motives that are immaterial in the administration of the law, the courts are not concerned with them. Malice, religious or other, may dictate a prosecution; but if the law has been violated, this fact never shields the law-breaker. Neither do the courts require that there shall be some moral obloquy to support a given law before enforcing it, and it is not necessary to maintain that to violate the Sunday observance custom [the act] shall be of itself immoral, to make it criminal in the eyes of the law. It may be harmless in itself (because, as petitioner believes, God has not set apart that day for rest and holiness) to work on Sunday; and yet, if man has set it apart, in due form, by his law, for rest, it must be obeyed as man's law if not as God's law; and it is just as evil to violate such a law, in the eyes of the world, as one sanctioned by God—I mean just as criminal in law. The crime is in doing the thing forbidden by law, harmless though it be in itself. [U. S. *vs.* Jackson, 25 Fed. Rep., 548; Re McCoy, 31, Fed. Rep., 794; S. C, 527, U. S. 731, 733.] Therefore, all that part of the argument that it is not hurtful in itself to work on Sunday, apart from the religious sanctity of the day, is beside the question; for it may be that the courts would hold that repeated repetitions of a violation of law forbidding even a harmless thing, could be a nuisance as tending to a breach of the peace. [2 Bish Cr. L., section 965; 1 Ib., section 812.] Neglecting to do a thing is sometimes a nuisance. [1 Russ. Cr., 318.] That is to say, a nuisance might be predicated of an act harmless in itself, if the will of the majority had lawfully forbidden the act, and rebellion against that will would be the *gravamen* of the offense; or to express it otherwise, there is in one sense a certain immorality in refusing obedience to the laws of one's country, subjection to which God himself has enjoined upon us.

But whatever plenary power may exist in the State to declare repeated violations of its laws and the usages of its people a nuisance and criminal, until the case of Parker *vs.* State, *supra,* and until this case of King, to which we yield our judicial obedience, there seems not to have been any law, statute or common, declaring the violation of the statutes against working on Sunday a common nuisance. Mr. Chief Justice Ruffin has demonstrated, we think, that there was no such common law of the mother State of North Carolina, from which we have derived our common law and these Sunday statutes. [M. & V. Code, 2,289, 2,009, 2,010, 2,011, 2,012, 2,013; Act N. C., 1,741; 1 Scott Rev., 55; Ib., 795; Car. & Nich., 638; State *vs.* Williams. 4 Ired., 400; State *vs.* Brooksbank, 6 Ired., 73.] The case of State *vs.* Lorry [7 Bax. 95] is in accordance with these authorities, and I may say that, with some patience, I have traced as far as I have been able the common law authorities, and if the judgment rested with me, should say that there is not any foundation in them for the ruling that it is a common law nuisance to work in one's fields on Sunday, and the Supreme Court of North Carolina so decided. Maul, J., said in Rawlins *vs.* West Derby [2 C. B. 74] that "in the time of Charles II, an Act of Parliament passed providing that certain things that formerly might have been done on Sunday should no longer be done on that day, all other things being left to the freedom of the common law."

This act was not adopted by North Carolina or by Tennessee as part of their common law, but was by North Carolina and afterward by Tennessee substantially re-enacted, and is the foundation of our Sunday laws. The [120] precedent for a common law indictment taken by Chitty from a manual known as the "Circuit Companion," was omitted from subsequent editions. [2 Chit. Cr., 6 Ed. 20 and note.] And while many American courts have laid hold of the statements in the old text writers, that such an indictment was known at common law, and upon their authority subsequent writers have proceeded to state the text law to be so, it is quite certain that no adjudicated case in England can be found to establish the statement that, strictly and technically, there was any such offense known to the common law. In this sense it may be said that King was wrongfully convicted, the State *vs.* Lorry wrongfully overruled, and Parker *vs.* State wrongfully decided; but it does not belong to this court to overrule these decisions, and it does belong to the State Court to make them, and King's conviction under them is "due process of law."

Remand the prisoner.

Declaration of Principles of the National Religious Liberty Association

• We believe in the religion taught by Jesus Christ.

• We believe in temperance and regard the liquor traffic as a curse to society.

• We believe in supporting the civil government, and submitting to its authority.

• We deny the right of any civil government to legislate on religious questions.

• We believe it is the right, and should be the privilege, of every man to worship according to the dictates of his own conscience.

• We also believe it to be our duty to use every lawful and honorable means to prevent religious legislation by the civil government that religious and civil liberty.

Adventist Pioneer Library

For more information, visit:
www.APLib.org

or write to:
contact@aplib.org

Made in the USA
Middletown, DE
16 June 2025

77027891R00070